ALVARO'S
MAMMA TOSCANA

ALVARO'S
MAMMA TOSCANA
THE AUTHENTIC TUSCAN COOKBOOK

ALVARO MACCIONI
PHOTOGRAPHS BY JAMES MURPHY

PAVILION

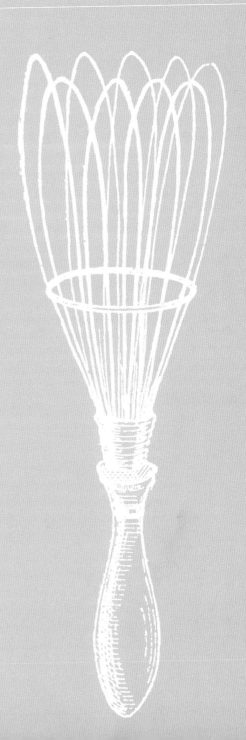

This edition first published in Great Britain in 2008

First published in Great Britain in 1998 by
Pavilion Books
An imprint of the Anova Books Group Ltd
10 Southcombe Street
LONDON W14 ORA

Designed by Isobel Gillan
Photography by James Murphy
Additional home economy by Allyson Birch

A CIP catalogue record for this book is available from the
British Library.

ISBN 9781862058545

Text set in Garamond

Printed in China by SNP Leefung

10 9 8 7 6 5 4 3 2 1

This book can be ordered direct from the publisher.
Please contact the Marketing Department. But try your
bookshop first.

www.anovabooks.com

CONTENTS

Introduction • 6

Soups • 8

Savouries • 22

Vegetables • 42

Pasta • 60

Poultry and Game • 82

Meat • 104

Fish and Shellfish • 136

Rice • 164

Sauces • 174

Desserts • 186

Index • 220

Acknowledgements • 224

INTRODUCTION

MY NAME IS ALVARO MACCIONI and I was born in Tuscany. If you lived in Tuscany before the Second World War, food was not as readily available as it is today in supermarkets and delicatessens. Instead, Mamma or Grandmamma went to the vegetable plot at the back of the house and found all the ingredients that could be used to make the dish for the day. We had to decide what was or was not edible from the grasses, herbs and roots growing in the garden. As I was growing up, I became more and more fascinated by food in general and by using all the vegetables and fruit which were readily available, and also in season. For example: in Italy, you cannot eat pork in the summer, only in the winter. Beef in those days was only for the rich and the little bit that we could get was the bit which no one used. We boiled it or put it in a stew. Steak was beyond our means. From necessity and poverty, we had to be inventive and we made dishes which today have become delicacies of Tuscan cuisine. In English, there is an old saying, 'necessity is the mother of invention.' In this book, you will find recipes from other mothers as well as my own. In many ways, because my mother was not always very well, I became the son of the whole village and was often invited to eat in the homes of my friends' families – this gave me many new ideas and inspired some of the recipes I use today.

As a young man, I decided that I wanted to work in catering. My father forced me to do something totally different and I attended agricultural college. In the last year of my studies there, I left school without my father's knowledge. By the time he realized that I wasn't at college any more, I was already studying catering at the Ecole Hôtelière in Lausanne, Switzerland. After two years, I graduated as a chef de partie: I was a trained cook, able to make sauces and to cook an international cuisine derived from the French.

As I grew up and worked in different places, I began to discover that everything considered to be civilized originated from the place I was born. Two thousand years before Christ, the Etruscans inhabited the area now known as Tuscany; they were the most civilized tribe in Europe.

And it is quite amazing to think that when the rest of the Continent was still firmly fixed in the medieval mindset, the Florentines were beginning to enjoy the benefits of the Renaissance.

In all the old palaces of Florence, you might have noticed that there is a little tower on the roof. We call this *piccionaia*, which means 'the pigeon-house'. At the time of the Medici, when there was certainly no air-conditioning, these pigeon houses were used as dining rooms, because you could only get fresh air on the rooftops. These dining rooms in the sky became a status symbol and they were used for special occasions. Today, we still use lots of recipes for dishes from those days. One example is Arista, which can be made from fillet of pork or wild boar (see page 128) It was served in 1250 at the meeting of the Ecumenical Council held in Florence. In those days, most of the Archbishops and Cardinals spoke Greek and in order to describe this fillet of roast pork as delicious, they said 'Aristo, aristo.' Aristo in Greek means 'fantastic' or 'well done'. Aristo became Arista, which is what the dish is now called. Many of my recipes date back to the 1100s – in catering we call it 'the beginning of time'. Another curious fact is that there are many theories about how the dish 'Bistecca alla Fiorentina' got its name. Some people say that the word 'bistecca' derives from beef steak. The actual truth is that 'bis' means double – fillet and entrecote. It is cooked on a picnic day called Festa del Grillo – the Feast of the Cricket – held on Ascension Day. Every family saves up to buy this famous cut of meat. A fire is lit in the Park of the Cascinea in Florence and the steak is stabbed on to a two-pronged wooden fork which is stuck into the ground; the meat is held in front of the fire in the same way as you would toast crumpets or muffins in England. This way the fat does not drip into the fire and make the meat smell of burning fat. The fat drips on to the ground and the meat is only slightly cooked; 'Bistecca alla Fiorentina' must always be very rare.

One could go on to discuss lots of different old recipes but what I have tried to do in this book is to present all the recipes cooked and prepared in the traditional Tuscan way. You have to remember that, because of our geographical position, Tuscan cuisine is the most varied in Italy. We have fish dishes deriving from the coast of Tuscany which starts from north of Rome and goes right into the Bay of Genoa. We have the Apennine mountains on our back, where dishes such as game, wild boar and polenta are still enjoyed. And please remember that Tuscany is the home of one of the oldest wines in the world – Chianti! Some savoury dishes are made with fruit and sweeteners such as honey and sweet wine. All the very old recipes from the time of Caterina de' Medici are sweetened with honey, marmalade and jam. These were used specifically to marinate meat – refrigeration was not available and they had, in some way, to counteract the smell of the meat which was hung for a week or more. It is said that food was practically invented in Tuscany! You can find recipes for fried chicken, sausages and fillet steak in antique recipe books dating back a thousand years or more. Cooking in the high society of Florence in the time of the Medici and the Borgia was entertainment – equivalent to what cinema, theatre and television are today. Even in paintings, unless they are religious ones, you will see depictions of food being prepared and cooked. It is very rare to read an old book from Tuscany on any kind of subject where at some stage there is not a description of a recipe or a banquet. The names of the artists of the Renaissance in Tuscany – Michelangelo, Raphael and so on – are very famous today, but we must remember that chefs were held in the same kind of esteem as artists, because the presentation of food (especially on special occasions) was thought to be a work of art. If you read any of these old books, you will find that even the way they slaughtered and skinned an animal was a work of art. And the people who made the pots and pans designed them like works of art because each pan was specially made to cook a particular dish. Today, chefs can become television stars, but, in fact, chefs have always been stars.

I would like to emphasize that 'Italian cuisine', as a lot of people call it, does not exist. In Italy, the cuisine is regional. You must remember that Italy, after all, only became a united country in the 1860s and in the mid-nineteenth century it was made up of 52 different states, with 19 different dialects. The only region which had been comparatively free of foreign influence was Tuscany and that is why Tuscan cuisine is now considered to be the most 'Italian'.

I have titled this book *Mamma Toscana,* not only because Mamma traditionally does the cooking, or even because I always say to the chefs in my restaurant, 'If you can cook like your mother, you are a great chef; if you can cook like your grandmother, you are even better,' but also because, for me, the mother figure represents Creation. Everything, from art to business, started in Italy. The first bank in Italy was also the first bank in the world, the Monte di Paschi di Siena, founded in 1413. This operated as pawn shops do today. In those days, the only collateral was cattle and sheep. The name means 'the hill of the pasture' that is, where the livestock could graze. When I teach at catering school in Tuscany, many foreign students ask me why all the famous Italians come from Tuscany: Michelangelo, Leonardo da Vinci, Raphael, Galileo Galilei. This is not because Tuscans are any cleverer than anyone else in Italy but because, in 1211, a law was passed which decreed that the first son of a non-servant family had to attend school. The rest of the world did not come to this idea until more than 500 years later.

But there is another side to Tuscany. It is said that, when God created the world, he looked at Italy and said I am supposed to be a just man but I have done two bad things: this beautiful boot in the middle of the Mediterranean sea is not fair on the rest of the world and Tuscany is the best part of the little boot.' To equal things out for the rest of the world, he put the Italians in the rest of Italy and the Toscani (Tuscan people) in Tuscany. Italy is the door to Heaven, Tuscany is Heaven, but because of the Tuscan people, it is just like the rest of the world!

ALVARO MACCIONI

SOUPS

SOUP IN ITALY DOES NOT ALWAYS MEAN SOUP. TO GIVE YOU AN EXAMPLE, WE CALL TRIFLE 'ENGLISH SOUP', ZUPPA INGLESE. IN TUSCANY, SOUP IS A WAY OF LIFE: AT LUNCH WE WILL EAT PASTA AS A STARTER AND THEN SOME SORT OF MAIN COURSE. DINNER IS ALWAYS SOUP FOLLOWED BY THE LEFTOVERS FROM LUNCH MASQUERADING IN A DIFFERENT GUISE. THE VARIETIES OF SOUP ARE INFINITE – WE MAKE SOUP WITH ALMOST ANYTHING, AS YOU WILL SEE FROM THE RECIPES I HAVE GIVEN. THE MOST FAMOUS SOUP IS RIBOLLITA, WHICH VARIES FROM TOWN TO TOWN IN TUSCANY. BASICALLY, IT IS A VEGETABLE SOUP, WITH BREAD, RE-HEATED (SEE PAGE 12).

PAPPA AL POMODORO

BREAD AND TOMATO SOUP

What can I say? I could write a book about this famous soup! The recipe varies from town to town and from family to family. We used to eat it on a Friday for dinner for two reasons: first, because as Roman Catholics we were not allowed to eat meat on a Friday, and secondly because bread made on a Saturday morning was supposed to last for seven days. On the seventh day, the stale bread would be used up in this soup. Many people confuse this with Aqua Cotta (see page 18) which is a broth, whereas this is quite thick and filling.

Serves 4

600g/1lb 6oz ripe tomatoes, skinned, de-seeded
   and sliced
olive oil
about 200g/7oz stale country-style bread
large fresh basil leaves
1 garlic clove, chopped
500ml/17fl oz/2½ cups stock or water
salt and freshly ground black pepper

To serve:
best-quality extra-virgin olive oil
freshly ground black pepper

Put the tomatoes in a saucepan with a little olive oil, the bread, basil, garlic and the stock or water. Season with salt and pepper. Bring to the boil and simmer, stirring frequently, until the bread is very soft, about 45 minutes. As the soup cooks, the bread will blend with the tomatoes, producing a soft, but not liquid, mixture.

Serve very hot, adding more salt, if necessary; dress with olive oil and freshly ground pepper.

ZUPPA DI PATATE

POTATO SOUP

My father was a potato eater – potatoes were his very favourite food. My mother would make this soup and put it in a flask for him to take to work for his lunch. Savoy potatoes are the best ones to use; if you can't find them, use a white-fleshed potato such as a King Edward.

Serves 4

1kg/2lb white-fleshed potatoes, such as King Edward
1 tbsp chopped fresh parsley
90ml/3fl oz/scant ½ cup olive oil
500g/1lb 2oz ripe tomatoes, skinned and chopped
1 onion, chopped
1 carrot, chopped
1 celery stick, chopped
salt and freshly ground black pepper

To serve:
butter, for frying
4 slices of stale bread
best-quality extra-virgin olive oil

Peel the potatoes and cut them into pieces. Cook them in 2 litres /3½ pints of salted, boiling water. Meanwhile, fry the parsley in the oil. As the potatoes start boiling, add the tomatoes, onion, carrot, celery and fried parsley. Bring back to the boil, season, cover and simmer for a further 1½ hours.

Push the vegetables and cooking liquid through a sieve into a clean saucepan; alternatively, liquidize or process it. The final texture is a matter of taste. Return to the heat and bring the soup to the boil again. Season with salt and pepper, as necessary.

Meanwhile, melt the butter in a frying-pan (skillet) and fry the bread until crisp and golden brown. Put a slice of bread in the bottom of each serving bowl and pour in the soup. Serve drizzled with a little olive oil.

GARMUGIA

SOUP OF MINCED (GROUND) BEEF, PANCETTA AND VEGETABLES

Serves 6

2 small globe artichokes
lemon juice
200g/7oz/4–6 asparagus spears
250g/9oz swiss chard, sliced
175ml/6fl oz/¾ cup olive oil
2 garlic cloves
1 onion, chopped
1 leek, chopped
1 celery stick, chopped
1 carrot, chopped
100g/4oz/¼ cup chopped pancetta or
    green (raw, uncured) belly of pork
500g/1lb 2oz minced (ground) beef
250g/9oz/½ cup shelled or frozen and
    thawed peas
3 litres/5¼ pints/12 cups vegetable stock
salt and freshly ground black pepper

To serve:
6 slices of country-style bread
grated parmesan cheese

This soup used to be served to weary pilgrims who took their rest in osterias *or inns as they travelled across Europe – the recipe can be traced back to 900AD. It would have been eaten from a wooden bowl with just a piece of bread to go with it. These days, what used to be simple rustic food has now become the height of chic, and you can find this in many a fashionable restaurant in Italy. In any case, it is wholesome, filling and simple to prepare.*

Prepare the artichokes. Remove and discard the hard outside leaves and the tops, so you end up with a stalk, heart and three-quarters of the tender leaves. Wash them and cut into segments. Peel the stalks. Slice the hearts and soak the slices in water, with a few drops of lemon juice, for 30 minutes.

Boil the asparagus in salted water; drain when only half-cooked.

Cook the swiss chard in just the water clinging to the leaves after washing. Squeeze the chard dry and then chop it finely.

Heat the olive oil in a large saucepan and fry the garlic, onion, leek, celery and carrot. Add the pancetta or pork belly and then the mince. Cook, stirring frequently to break up the mince, until the mince is well browned. Add all the other vegetables, season with salt and pepper to taste and pour on enough stock to cover. Simmer for 1 hour, adding more stock as necessary to keep it moist, at regular intervals.

After an hour, pour in the remaining stock and continue simmering for a further 30 minutes.

To serve, toast the bread, then place the slices of toasted bread in serving bowls. Add salt and pepper to the garmugia, if necessary, and spoon the soup over the bread.

You can add grated parmesan cheese and more black pepper for extra flavour, if you like.

RIBOLLITA

VEGETABLE SOUP

Serves 4

500g/1lb 2oz/1¼ cups fresh canellini beans,
    shelled, or 250g/9oz/generous ½ cup
    dried beans
75ml/3fl oz/scant ½ cup extra-virgin olive oil
1 onion, chopped
1 carrot, chopped
1 celery stick, chopped
2 tbsp chopped fresh parsley
pinch of chopped fresh thyme
small piece of fresh root ginger, peeled and
    chopped
1–2 black cabbages or 225g/8oz/2 cups curly
    kale, shredded
savoy cabbage, shredded
1 medium-large tomato, skinned and chopped
thin slices of country-style white or brown bread
salt

To serve:
1 onion, finely chopped
best-quality extra-virgin olive oil
freshly ground black pepper

It is almost a contradiction in terms to give a recipe for ribollita (the name literally means 'boiled over') since, as the name suggests, the dish is none other than the leftovers of the vegetable soup from the night before, boiled again, with added bread and olive oil. However, the dish is so utterly delicious that it is worth making from scratch, without waiting for leftovers. You can use any seasonal vegetables you like, such as courgettes (zucchini), french (green) beans, potatoes and so on.

If using dried beans, soak them overnight. The next day, rinse them and boil them in plenty of fresh boiling water for 1½ hours, or until soft. Add salt near the end of cooking.

If using fresh beans, cook them in plenty of boiling water for about 35 minutes.

When the beans are ready, push them through a fairly wide sieve, with their cooking liquid. You could also use a liquidizer or food processor to purée them.

Heat the oil in a large, heavy saucepan and fry the onion, carrot, celery, herbs and spices. Add both the black cabbage or kale and the savoy cabbage and cook for a further 10 minutes.

Stir in the cooked beans, the tomato and salt. Add water to cover generously. Cook for about 2 hours.

Arrange a layer of bread in another saucepan. Pour a few ladlefuls of vegetable soup over the bread and repeat until you have used up all the ingredients. Cover and let stand for several hours.

Bring back to the boil, sprinkling a finely chopped onion, a generous helping of olive oil and black pepper on top to serve.

ZUPPA DI MAGRO GRASSO

PUMPKIN SOUP

Serves 6

500g/1lb 2oz/1¼ cups fresh borlotti beans,
    shelled, or 250g/9oz/generous ½ cup dried
    beans
1 ham bone, washed
50g/2oz/⅛ cup chopped pancetta or green
    (raw, uncured) belly of pork
1 onion (¼–½ cup), chopped
1 celery stick, chopped
1 carrot, chopped
2 garlic cloves, chopped
1 tbsp chopped fresh parsley
1 tbsp chopped fresh borage
300g/11oz black cabbage or curly kale, sliced
200g/7oz pumpkin, peeled, de-seeded and
    diced
300g/11oz ripe tomatoes, skinned and diced,
    or canned peeled tomatoes
salt and freshly ground black pepper

To serve:
6 slices of country-style bread
best-quality extra-virgin olive oil
freshly ground black pepper

As a little boy, I can remember looking out of the window and seeing the fog resting on the Tuscan hills and the rain steaming up the glass of the window as my grandmother prepared this delicious soup. The name magro grasso *means 'thin and fat'. It is so called because it is a vegetable soup, cooked with a very little pancetta and with stock made from a ham bone, so it has a meaty flavour but without any large pieces of meat.*

If using dried beans, soak them overnight in plenty of cold water. The next day, drain and rinse them, then cook them with the ham bone, in fresh boiling water to cover amply, for about 1½ hours, or until soft. Add salt towards the end of cooking.

If using fresh beans, cook them in plenty of slightly salted boiling water for about 35 minutes, with the ham bone.

When the beans are almost ready, fry the pancetta or belly of pork in a large earthenware casserole or a heavy-based, flameproof casserole until the fat runs; then fry the onion, celery, carrots, garlic and herbs in the fat, until soft.

Blanch the cabbage leaves for a few minutes in boiling water. Drain, then add them, with the pumpkin and tomatoes, to the casserole. Season with salt and pepper and stew the vegetables, sprinkling with the cooking water from the beans when necessary, until they are cooked, about 30 minutes.

When both the beans and vegetables are ready, remove the ham bone from the beans and mix the beans, their cooking water and the vegetables together. Cook for a further 20–25 minutes.

Place the slices of bread in serving bowls, pour the soup on top and serve with olive oil and freshly ground black pepper.

MINESTRA DI FARRO

THE MILLER'S SOUP

Serves 6

250g/9oz spelt or other whole wheat grains
250g/9oz/generous ½ cup dried beans
150g/5oz/¾ cup chopped pancetta or green
  (raw, uncured) belly of pork
1 onion, chopped
1 carrot, chopped
1 celery stick, chopped
2 garlic cloves
1 tsp tomato purée (paste), diluted in a little
  warm water
3 leaves of black cabbage or curly kale, sliced
2 litres/3½ pints/8⅔ cups water
salt and freshly ground black pepper

To serve:
best-quality extra-virgin olive oil
freshly ground black pepper

This is a soup that the Romans used to eat and which you can find mentioned in history books. As they had no potatoes in those days, they used wheat to add thickness. My family used to eat this on cold, snowy days in winter. The word farro *means spelt, an ancient type of wheat that is becoming popular again. You can use any kind of whole wheat grains, which are available from healthfood shops.*

Soak the spelt overnight in plenty of cold water. Soak the beans overnight in enough water to cover them generously.

The next day, drain and rinse the spelt and then cook it in plenty of water for at least 3 hours. Drain and rinse the beans.

Fry the pancetta or pork belly in a large saucepan for a few minutes. Then add the onion, carrot, celery and garlic. Sauté until the garlic is brown; then remove the cloves. Pour in the diluted tomato purée (paste) and simmer for 5 minutes.

Add the cabbage or kale and cook until wilted. Now add the beans and water and simmer for a further 1½ hours.

Drain and stir in the spelt and cook for about 15 minutes, to allow all the flavours to blend well. Season to taste.

Dish out into soup bowls and dress with olive oil and black pepper.

ZUPPA DEI MORI

SOUP OF THE MOORS

So called after the Arabs of Spain, this soup resembles gazpacho. My auntie used to make it very well, but we used to tease her that she was the 'intruder' in our family because she was the wife of a Sicilian. When I grew up – guess what? I married a Sicilian and she refreshed my memory about this wonderful summer soup. Make it the day before, keep it in the fridge and eat it cold.

Serves 6

½ cucumber, peeled and cubed
1 fennel bulb, sliced thinly
1 celery heart, chopped
1 head of cos lettuce, chopped
4 tomatoes, peeled, de-seeded and chopped
3 carrots, quartered
3 garlic cloves, chopped
1 lemon, peeled and sliced thinly
1 dried red chilli, chopped
generous bunch of fresh basil
75ml/3fl oz/scant ½ cup extra-virgin olive oil
salt and freshly ground black pepper

To serve:
best-quality extra-virgin olive oil
lemon juice
croûtons (optional)

Put all the vegetables, the garlic, the flesh and juice of the lemon, the chilli, basil and olive oil in a food processor and process until finely chopped into about 5mm/½-inch pieces. Add a tumbler of water and season with salt and pepper. Process briefly, to mix. Transfer to a soup tureen or serving bowl and chill until required. Dress the soup with olive oil and lemon juice to taste and serve with croûtons, if you like.

ZUPPA DI POLLO

CHICKEN SOUP

This is a chicken soup that is also known as 'Grandmother's Soup'. Until I grew up, I was under the impression that this soup had medicinal purposes: I was always given it when I was unwell. Risotto is often made using this soup as a base.

Serves 6

For the broth:
1.2kg/2lb 12oz chicken, cut into joints
1 large onion, 1 large carrot, 1 celery stick, roughly chopped
salt

To serve:
75ml/3fl oz/scant ½ cup extra-virgin olive oil
1 small onion, chopped
1 small carrot, chopped
½ celery stick, chopped
salt and freshly ground black pepper

To make the broth
Put the chicken in a large earthenware or other heavy-based flameproof casserole, with the onion, carrot and celery stick, and cover with plenty of cold water. Add salt and bring to the boil. Cook for about 35 minutes, until the chicken can easily be pulled apart.

Remove the chicken, reserving the stock but discarding the vegetables. When cool enough to handle, skin, bone and mince (grind) the chicken.

To finish the soup
Heat the olive oil in an earthenware or other heavy-based flameproof casserole and fry the chopped onion, carrot and celery stick until just browned.

Stir in the minced chicken. Season well and add enough of the reserved chicken stock to cover. Bring to the boil and cook for a few minutes before serving.

AQUA COTTA

COOKED WATER SOUP

When I was growing up in Tuscany during the war there was no petrol for transport, so produce such as wood, olives and grapes were often carried by horse and cart. I remember one particular man who, when he stopped to rest, used to give his horse water from a bucket. He would then boil water and bread in the very same bucket and make this soup for his lunch.

Serves 4

75ml/3fl oz/scant ½ cup extra-virgin olive oil
2 onions, thinly sliced
350g/12oz red or yellow (bell) peppers, cored, de-seeded and sliced
2 celery sticks, sliced
500g/1lb 2oz ripe tomatoes, skinned and puréed
salt and freshly ground black pepper
1 litre/1¾ pints/4¼ cups water
4 eggs
4 slices of country-style bread
2 tbsp grated parmesan cheese

Heat the oil in a flameproof earthenware dish or a heavy-based saucepan and fry the onions until softened. Add the peppers and celery and fry for 5 minutes; then stir in the tomatoes. Season with salt and pepper and cook for a further 20 minutes,

Add the water. Bring to the boil and cook for about 5 minutes.

Meanwhile, beat the eggs in a bowl large enough to contain the vegetables; season. Toast the bread and place slices of toasted bread in the serving bowls.

Pour the vegetables over the eggs, stir and leave for a minute or so, until the hot liquid lightly cooks the eggs. Pour over the toasted bread in the serving bowls and sprinkle with parmesan.

ZUPPA PAESANA

FARMHOUSE SOUP

We used to eat this hearty, filling soup as a mid-week meal with some bread. My mother would make it with any vegetables and leftovers she had in the kitchen. It will feed four starving-hungry people or maybe a few more with lesser appetites!

Serves 4

450g/1lb/1 cup fresh cannellini or borlotti
  beans, shelled, or 225/8oz/½ cup
  dried beans
¼ savoy cabbage
150g/5oz fresh spinach
6 swiss chard leaves or dark green
  lettuce leaves
50g/2oz/⅛ cup chopped prosciutto or
  unsmoked back bacon
25g/1oz finely chopped fresh parsley
1 garlic clove, finely chopped
1 carrot, cut into thin strips
1 potato, peeled and cut into thin strips
1 celery stick, cut into thin strips
2 strips of belly pork, cubed
1 tbsp tomato purée (paste), diluted with a little
  very hot water
2 litres/3½ pints/8⅔ cups meat stock
salt and freshly ground black pepper
250g/9oz long-grain rice

To serve:
2 heaped tbsp grated parmesan cheese

If you are using dried beans, cover them with cold water and soak overnight. Then drain and rinse. Boil them twice for 10 minutes in plenty of fresh water, draining and rinsing them in between each boiling. Cover them in fresh cold water, bring to the boil, then cover tightly and simmer for an hour or until tender. Drain.

If you are using fresh beans, shell them, cover with cold water and simmer for an hour or until tender. Drain.

Shred all the green vegetables together. Place in a saucepan with a little water and cook until just soft, about 5 minutes. Remove from the heat, cool and then squeeze dry in your fists.

Place the prosciutto or bacon in a big cast-iron or heavy-based saucepan, with the parsley and the garlic. Fry together gently for about 5 minutes (you don't need to add extra oil: the fat from the prosciutto is enough). Add the green vegetables to the prosciutto, parsley and garlic, stir together, then add all the other vegetables, the belly pork and the beans. Stir in the diluted tomato purée (paste) and the stock, cover and leave to simmer for about 2 hours. The final consistency should be very creamy.

Check the seasoning and add salt and pepper if required. Add the rice, stir well and continue to cook for about 15–20 minutes or until the rice is tender. Remove from the heat and stir in the parmesan cheese. Serve hot or cold but not chilled.

PASTA E CECI

PASTA AND CHICKPEA SOUP

*Although this is not so common in Italian restaurants
in London, it is as popular a dish in Italian trattoria
as Pasta e Fagioli (see right). It is also one of the oldest
recipes on record: there is evidence that the Romans
used to eat it. As a child I never liked chickpeas, but
now I love to eat this soup! You really must use
rosemary – no other herb will do.*

Serves 4

250g/9oz dried chickpeas
salt
2 garlic cloves, chopped
2 tbsp olive oil
1 fresh rosemary sprig
1 tsp tomato purée (paste), diluted in 90ml/3fl oz/scant cup
  warm water
150g/5oz tagliatelle, broken into pieces

Soak the chickpeas overnight.

Rinse the chickpeas and cook in plenty of lightly
salted water for 35 minutes. Drain, reserving the
cooking water.

In an earthenware or other heavy-based flameproof
casserole, brown the garlic in the oil, then add the
rosemary and the diluted tomato purée (paste).

Sieve, liquidize or process two-thirds of the
chickpeas to a purée and pour these and the whole
chickpeas into the casserole. Cook the pasta in the
chickpea cooking liquid and drain when *al dente*.
Add them to the casserole and serve.

PASTA E FAGIOLI

THICK BEAN SOUP

*I used to feel a sense of festivity when eating this
elegant soup, because it was always served on special
feast days. Mamma would add the pasta – fresh pasta,
not the little tubes which are generally served in the
rest of Italy – five minutes before the end. The best
shape of pasta to use is macaroni.*

Serves 6

450g/1lb/1 cup fresh cannellini or borlotti beans, shelled,
  or 225g/8oz/$^1/_2$ cup dried beans
75ml/3fl oz/scant $^1/_2$ cup olive oil
4 garlic cloves, chopped
1.5 litres/3 pints/6 cups cold water
1 tbsp tomato purée (paste)
salt and freshly ground black pepper
3 fresh rosemary sprigs, tied together
325g/12oz dried or fresh pasta of a short, stubby shape,
  e.g. macaroni

If using dried beans, soak them in cold water for
24 hours. Drain the beans, rinse well and boil quickly
in fresh water for 5 minutes. Drain and reserve.

If using fresh beans, cook them in boiling, slightly
salted water for about 35 minutes.

Heat the oil in a heavy-based saucepan and fry the
garlic until it is well browned; then add the beans.
Stir together and cover with cold water. Cover and
simmer slowly for about 1$^1/_2$ hours, or until the beans
are tender.

Stir in the tomato purée (paste), season with salt
and pepper, and add the rosemary. Simmer for about
10 minutes. Then add the pasta, making sure there is
enough liquid to cook the pasta; add more boiling
water if necessary. Simmer until the pasta is ready and
then serve, removing the bunch of rosemary first.

SAVOURIES

TUSCANY ENJOYS THE BEST CLIMATE IN WHICH TO GROW VEGETABLES, MAIZE AND FRUIT, SO MOST TUSCAN DISHES ARE MADE WITH VEGETABLES, OLIVE OIL AND BREAD – THE PRODUCE OF THE FARM. ONE OF THE REASONS WHY TUSCANY HAS ONE OF THE WIDEST MENUS IN ITALY IS BECAUSE OF ITS GEOGRAPHICAL POSITION: IT HAS THE SEA, THE MOUNTAINS, THE VALLEYS AND THE PLAINS SO, EVEN BEFORE MODERN FARMING METHODS CAME TO EUROPE, WE COULD GROW ANYTHING.

FOCACCIA

SMALL THIN PIZZAS

Makes 16

450g/1lb/3½ cups semolina flour
350g/12½ oz/3 cups unbleached plain
   (all-purpose) white flour
50g/2oz fresh compressed yeast or
   4 x 15g sachets active dry yeast
450ml/16fl oz/2 cups lukewarm water,
   depending on the yeast
2 tsp coarse-grained salt

To serve:
extra-virgin olive oil
fine sea salt

Focaccia *is the bread eaten for breakfast in Tuscany. It can be eaten on its own or split and filled, like a sandwich. A little fact that everyone ought to know: before pizza was ever called pizza, it was called* foccacine *and derived from Arab unleavened bread. Under Moorish occupation, the Italians thought to add something to flavour the dough, but as this was before Christopher Columbus had discovered America, there were no tomatoes. So the dough was flavoured with olive oil, salt, rosemary or sage. When tomatoes arrived in Italy in 1700, a sauce was made with garlic, oregano, capers and garlic – and tomatoes. This sauce was known as* pizzaiola *and was put on top of the unleavened bread.*

Mix the semolina flour and the plain (all-purpose) flour together, place in a mound on a board and make a well in the centre. Dissolve the yeast in a cup of the water, with most of the salt, and pour it into the well of the flour. Start mixing with a wooden spoon, incorporating some of the flour from the edges as well. When a rather thick batter is formed, add a second cup of salted water to the well and keep working with the spoon, incorporating more flour. When a dough is formed, start kneading with your hands, until all but ¼ cup of the flour is incorporated.

Divide the dough into 16 pieces. Using the remaining flour to prevent the dough from sticking, knead each piece for 30 seconds. Form into rounds, then arrange on trays. Cover the trays with clean teatowels and leave to rest in a warm place, away from draughts, until doubled in size – about an hour.

When ready, roll out the focaccia, one at a time, with a rolling pin; the dough should not be more than 5mm/½ inch thick. Let the focaccia rest again, covered with teatowels, in a warm place, away from draughts, until doubled in size – about an hour. Meanwhile, preheat the oven to 200°C/400°F/Gas Mark 6. The breads can be baked on a pizza stone or a cast-iron baking tray.

Sprinkle the focaccia with the remaining salt and bake them, one or more at a time, according to the capacity of your oven, for 4–5 minutes on each side, until crisp.

Remove from the oven, pour some olive oil all over and sprinkle with salt. Serve hot.

TORTA DI CARCIOFI

BAKED ARTICHOKE CAKE

We used to eat meat maybe once a week or twice at the most. This is why torta was made without meat. When artichokes were abundant we used to make this in many different ways. It is like an omelette and you can put it inside focaccia and take it on picnics. I love it very much. If you want, you can replace the artichokes with courgettes, boiled cardoons or aubergines.

Serves 6

12 globe artichokes, as tender as you can find
lemon juice
4 garlic cloves, crushed
90ml/3fl oz/scant ½ cup olive oil
2 tbsp chopped fresh parsley
5 eggs, beaten
salt and freshly ground black pepper

Remove and discard all the hard exterior leaves and the spiky tips of the artichokes, so you end up with a stalk, heart and three-quarters of the tender leaves. Peel the stalks until you get to the tender part and then cut the artichokes lengthways in thin slices and soak them in cold water, to which you have added some lemon juice, for 30 minutes.

Preheat the oven to 200°C/400°F/Gas Mark 6. Fry the garlic in the oil until golden. Remove the garlic and add the artichoke slices. When cooked, add the parsley.

Place the cooked artichokes in an ovenproof dish with their own cooking juices. Spoon the beaten eggs over them, season and bake until the eggs are set but not completely dry, about 15 minutes (but watch it carefully to judge when it is ready). Serve hot or cold.

LE CIACCE FRITTE

FRIED PIZZAS

In Tuscany we always treasure bread when it is hot. When I was a little boy, I remember crying one morning because I didn't want to take a slice of cold bread to school, so Mamma made me these special ciacce fritte *which she wrapped for me while they were piping hot. They are little focaccia which can be cut in two and filled with prosciutto or salami. You can also sprinkle them with sugar and eat them as a pudding.*

bread dough (see Focaccia, page 24)
olive oil, for shallow-frying
salt or sugar, to serve

Using a rolling pin, roll out the bread dough into rounds to fit your frying-pan (skillet) and to a thickness of about 3mm/⅛ inch.

Put plenty of oil in the frying-pan (skillet) and heat it up until very hot. Fry the dough discs until golden and serve sprinkled with either salt or sugar.

CROSTINI CON FEGATINI DI POLLO

CHICKEN-LIVER TOASTS

Every Tuscan mother makes this dish. If you are invited to Sunday lunch or indeed to any feast in a house, crostini will be served at the beginning of the meal. It is the most popular antipasto in Tuscany, more so than bruschetta or salami. There are, of course, variations, but chicken liver is the most favoured topping. Put the topping on small slices of country-style bread or, if you can get hold of it, on slices of frusta da crostini, *a soft, white bread with a glossy crust.*

Serves 8

90ml/3fl oz/scant ½ cup olive oil
1 leek, white part only, finely chopped
2 celery sticks, finely chopped
300g/11oz chicken livers, trimmed, washed (do not forget to
   remove the bile sack) and cut into chunks
200 ml/7fl oz/scant 1 cup dry white wine
150g/5oz capers, rinsed and finely chopped
hot chicken stock
salt and freshly ground black pepper
small slices of country-style bread or frusta da crostini, toasted

Heat most of the oil in a frying-pan (skillet) and sauté the leek and celery until golden. Add the chicken livers, season with salt and pepper and fry for a few minutes.

Sprinkle with the wine and stir with a wooden spoon, scraping the bottom of the pan, until the wine has evaporated.

Add the capers and cook for a further 15 minutes, stirring the whole time and adding a little hot stock from time to time to keep the mixture moist. Bear in mind, however, that the dish must not be runny, but quite thick.

Remove from the heat, lift out the chicken livers and chop them finely. Return them to the pan, add a little more olive oil and cook over a very low heat, stirring until you have a thick and creamy mixture.

Spread on slices of toasted bread and try to serve very hot.

POLENTA DI FAGIOLI E CAVOLO

POLENTA WITH BEANS AND CABBAGE

This is a very wholesome winter dish which we used to eat on a Friday. Porridge is said to keep you warm: this will keep you warmer. When you eat it I promise you will want nothing else.

Serves 6

400g/14oz/1 cup fresh cannellini or borlotti beans, shelled, or
    200g/7oz/½ cup dried beans
1.4 litres/2 pints/6¼ cups water
50g/2oz green (unsmoked, uncured) belly of pork or streaky bacon
1 onion, chopped
1 carrot, chopped
1 celery stick, chopped
1 leek (white part only), chopped
bouquet garni of fresh thyme, parsley, basil and rosemary sprigs
50g/2oz lard
300g/11oz black cabbage or curly kale, chopped
1 tbsp tomato purée (paste), diluted in 125ml/4fl oz/½ cup warm water
500g/1lb 2oz/3 cups polenta
salt and freshly ground black pepper

If using dried beans, soak them overnight in plenty of water. The next day, drain and rinse the beans and cook in plenty of boiling water, with the belly of pork or bacon, until soft, about 1½ hours. Add salt towards the end of cooking.

If using fresh beans, cook them in slightly salted water, with the belly of pork or bacon, for about 35 minutes or until soft.

While the beans are cooking, fry the onion, carrot, celery, leek and bouquet garni in the lard until softened. Stir into the beans and their cooking water when these are about two-thirds into their cooking time. Add the cabbage and the diluted tomato purée (paste) and season with salt and pepper, if necessary. Cover and cook until the vegetables are done, about 10 minutes. Remove the pork or bacon.

At this point, trickle in the polenta like light rain and cook for a further 45 minutes, stirring frequently with a wooden spoon to prevent lumps from forming.

Serve hot, warm or cold. Once it is cold, you can slice it and fry it in oil.

FRITTATA CON PANCETTA

BACON OMELETTE

This simple omelette is the most popular filling for Focaccia (see page 24).

Serves 4

6 eggs
400g/14oz pancetta or bacon, diced
1 tbsp olive oil
salt and freshly ground black pepper

In a bowl, beat the eggs and season with salt and pepper. Sauté the pancetta in a frying-pan (skillet) and then pour in the beaten eggs. Fry over a medium heat, turning the omelette over when it is set.

Slide on to a serving dish, cut into segments and serve at once.

FRITTATA DI BIETOLE

SWISS CHARD OMELETTE

Let me tell you that in Italy our main meal is lunch. Frittata (omelette) is often eaten for our evening meal, as we only want a small dinner then. If we stay out late, then we eat pizza. Incidentally, swiss chard is the most authentic filling that is used for pasta – although now you are more likely to see it filled with spinach.

Serves 4

400g/14oz swiss chard
2 tbsp olive oil
6 eggs
50g/2oz prosciutto (ham), some lean and some fat, chopped
salt and freshly ground black pepper

Clean the swiss chard, discarding the hard parts, and cut the leaves into big chunks. Rinse, then cook in just the water clinging to the leaves for about 8 minutes. Drain, squeeze dry, then sauté in a frying-pan (skillet) in the olive oil. Season with salt and pepper.

Meanwhile, beat the eggs in a bowl with some more salt and pepper. Stir in the prosciutto.

As soon as the chard is hot and sizzling, pour in the egg mixture. Fry over a medium heat, turning the omelette over when set.

Slide on to a serving dish, cut into segments and serve at once.

FRITTATA ALLA CONTADINA

FARMHOUSE OMELETTE

This is an omelette that Mamma made quite often. I used to like eating it inside Focaccia (see page 24).

Serves 4

6 eggs
1 tbsp plain (all-purpose) white flour
1 tbsp olive oil
salt and freshly ground black pepper

For the sauce:
2 tbsp olive oil
1 onion, finely chopped
1 carrot, finely chopped
1 celery stick, finely chopped
1 tbsp chopped fresh parsley
300g/11oz ripe tomatoes, skinned,
    de-seeded and puréed

First, make the sauce: put the oil in a frying-pan (skillet) and fry the onion, carrot, celery and parsley. Add the tomatoes, season and cook for a further 15 minutes.

Beat the eggs in a bowl with the flour and some salt and pepper.

Put a little olive oil in a clean frying-pan (skillet), heat and pour in the egg mixture. Fry over a medium heat, turning the omelette over when it is set. Slide the omelette on a plate to cool down a little; then cut it into squares.

Add the omelette squares to the sauce, gently stir everything together to blend all the flavours and then serve at once.

TORTA DI CECI

CHICKPEA CAKE

This was my grandmother's speciality and my grandfather was very fond of eating it. He used to cut it into little pieces, leaving one large piece, and say, 'Lucky are the last if the first are honest!' In that way, he would always get the biggest piece. You can eat this either hot or cold.

Serves 6

250g/9oz/1½ cups chickpea flour
100ml/3½ fl oz/scant ½ cup olive oil
salt and freshly ground black pepper

Dilute the flour in a bowl in just under 1 litre/1¾ pints/4½ cups of water. Let it lie on the bottom of the bowl for an hour.

Preheat the oven to 180°C/350°F/Gas Mark 4. Stir the chickpea flour with a palette knife. Stir in the oil and a pinch of salt.

Grease a shallow, ovenproof dish (bearing in mind that the mixture must not be more than 5mm/¼ inch deep when spread in the dish). Pour in the chickpea mixture. Bake in the oven until golden, about 25–30 minutes.

Sprinkle with black pepper and serve cut into slices.

VERDE FRITTO

MIXED VEGETABLE FRITTERS

In Florence we tend to fry many dishes. This is a mixture of vegetables, deep-fried in batter, which should be served as a starter, put in the centre of the table and followed by pasta. In Italy a fritto misto *is the generic name for an assortment of fried vegetables and shouldn't contain meat or fish unless it is specifically called* fritto misto di carne *or* di pesce. *I have invented a new name to avoid confusion, so that people know that it contains only vegetables.*

Serves 6

6 small globe artichokes
lemon juice
6 vegetable marrow flowers (only the flowers) or courgette flowers
6 small courgettes (zucchini)
2 eggs
225g/8oz/2 cups plain (all-purpose) white flour, plus extra for coating
1 tbsp milk
salt and freshly ground black pepper
olive oil for deep-frying

Remove and discard all the hard exterior leaves of the artichokes and cut the hardest tips off. Peel the stalks until you get to the tender heart and cut the artichokes into segments. Soak them in lemon juice for 30 minutes.

Remove the petals of the flowers and cut the stalks in two.

Cut the courgettes (zucchini) in half and de-seed them. Cut them into chips about 5cm/2 inches by 5mm/^{1}/$_4$ inch by 5mm/^{1}/$_4$ inch.

Beat the eggs with the flour, the milk and some salt and pepper, so as to obtain a liquid batter. Heat the oil for deep-frying until it is very hot; a cube of day-old bread should brown in about 30 seconds.

Dip the courgettes, marrow flowers and artichokes in the batter. Shake them gently to let any excess batter drip off. It is better to fry the different vegetables separately, reheating the oil between each batch. Deep-fry for a few minutes, until crisp and brown. Put the fritters to drain on kitchen paper and keep them warm while you fry the rest. Serve hot.

LA SCHIACCIATA

SAGE AND ROSEMARY BREAD

A traditional custom in old country kitchens was to make a few small sweet ones when the savoury schiacciata *was in preparation, to keep the children happy. If you, too, want to get into your children's good books, simply substitute sugar for the salt and garnish with sultanas rather than sage. If you go to a bar in Florence, you will be offered* schiacciata *to eat with your coffee.*

Makes 1 schiacciata

1kg/2lb bread dough (see Focaccia, page 24)
fresh sage and rosemary leaves
sea salt
olive oil

Preheat the oven to 200°C/400°F/Gas Mark 6. Put the dough on a worktop and, pressing down with your fingertips, flatten it out into a round about 1cm/^{1}/$_2$ inch thick.

Place the dough on a lightly greased baking sheet. Scatter it with sage and rosemary leaves, sprinkle it with salt and a little oil and bake for about 20 minutes.

PANZANELLA

TOMATO AND BREAD SALAD

We used to eat this salad with olive oil on a hot summer's day under the shade of a fig tree, all of us sitting on wooden benches round a wooden table. It is a good example of how bread is used in Tuscany. We use it in soup, to make pasta sauces, and in this case, in a salad. It is best to use ciabatta bread that is one day old and not too fresh.

Serves 4

5 ripe tomatoes
5 slices of 1-day-old ciabatta bread, cubed
½ cucumber, peeled and sliced
5 spring onions, sliced
bunch of fresh basil
1 tbsp wine vinegar
3 tbsp extra-virgin olive oil
salt and freshly ground black pepper

De-seed the tomatoes and place the seeds in a bowl. Place the ciabatta bread cubes in the bowl with the tomato seeds and mix, so that the bread soaks up the juice and seeds. If there is not sufficient juice, add a little water.

Chop the rest of the de-seeded tomatoes and put them in a salad bowl. Add the cucumber, spring onions and the fresh basil leaves.

Take the soaked ciabatta bread and, if it is too wet, squeeze out any excess liquid. Add to the salad bowl. Add the wine vinegar and olive oil and season with salt and pepper to taste. Toss the salad and serve.

PEPERONATA

GRILLED PEPPER (BELL PEPPER) SALAD

Mamma would use this as a sauce for pasta or for meat, such as veal and chicken, and also as a filling for Focaccia (see page 24). It will keep for 3 or 4 days in the fridge. To serve as a salad, you could add black olives and sprinkle with freshly chopped parsley.

Serves 4

6 large green, red and yellow peppers (bell peppers)
6 garlic cloves, halved
1 large onion, chopped
225ml/8fl oz/1 cup olive oil
350g/12oz prosciutto crudo (raw cured ham), cut into strips
1 carrot, finely chopped
900g/2lb tomatoes, peeled, de-seeded and chopped
1 tsp sugar
salt
paprika

Preheat the grill until very hot. To peel the peppers: put them under the grill until the skins char. Plunge into cold water and, when cool enough to handle, rub off the skins with paper towels.

Meanwhile, sweat the garlic and onion in the oil in a frying-pan (skillet). When soft but not coloured, add the ham.

Slice the peppers, take out the seeds and place the peppers in the frying-pan, stirring well. Cook for 5 minutes.

Add the carrot, tomatoes and sugar and season with salt and paprika. Simmer until you have a thick, stew-like mixture. Serve in an earthenware dish, if possible.

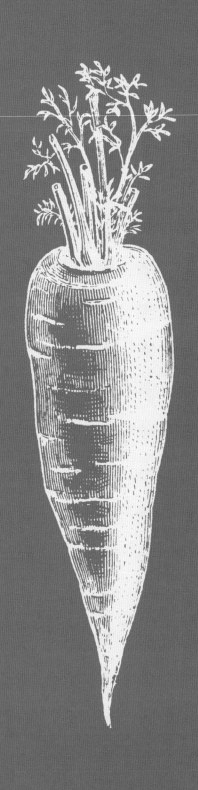

VEGETABLES

TUSCAN CUISINE IS SEASONAL. TUSCAN FAMILIES WOULD NEVER DREAM OF SERVING ASPARAGUS AT CHRISTMAS, BECAUSE WE BELIEVE THAT EVERY VEGETABLE THAT GROWS IN TUSCANY HAS BEEN KISSED BY GOD: THIS IS WHY WE ONLY EAT VEGETABLES WHEN THEY ARE IN SEASON – THE FLAVOUR OF GOD'S KISS WILL DISAPPEAR OTHERWISE. SO ALL THESE DISHES ARE BEST MADE WHEN THE INGREDIENTS ARE IN SEASON. IN WINTER, AS THERE ARE SO FEW FRESH INGREDIENTS, WE USE A LOT OF DRIED BEANS, LENTILS, AND PEAS, RATHER THAN USING SOMETHING THAT IS GROWN OUT OF SEASON. WHEN I WAS A BOY DURING THE WAR, WE WERE FORCED TO BE VEGETABLE EATERS BECAUSE THERE WAS LITTLE ELSE TO EAT. WE HAD TO FIND DIFFERENT WAYS OF COOKING VEGETABLES TO MAKE LIFE MORE INTERESTING. ALMOST EVERYBODY HAD A GARDEN IN THOSE DAYS AND, UNLIKE IN ENGLAND, VERY FEW FLOWERS WERE GROWN. INSTEAD WE GREW THE VEGETABLES THAT WE COOKED AND ATE – THE GARDEN WAS PART OF THE HOUSEHOLD ECONOMY OF THE FAMILY. SOME OF THESE RECIPES CAN ALSO BE USED AS PASTA SAUCES, SUCH AS STUFATO DI PISELLI (SEE PAGE 48) AND FAGIOLINI ALLA FIORENTINA (SEE PAGE 45).

CIPOLLE ALLA GROSSETANA

TUSCAN STUFFED ONIONS

When I was little, I used to hate onions – this was the dish that converted me! I was a big meat eater, so the first time I ate this I thought the onions were meatballs; I noticed that the taste was a little strange, but it was so delicious that I ate them anyway. In the old days, it would have been eaten as a main course. Today it is used as a garnish.

Serves 4

8 onions
15g/½ oz dried porcini mushrooms
25g/1oz/2 tbsp butter
100g/4oz minced (ground) veal
100g/4oz *salsiccia* (Italian sausage), skinned and chopped
1 egg
salt, pepper and grated nutmeg

Peel the onions and boil them for approximately 10 minutes in salted water. Drain. Carefully scoop out the insides of the onions and chop them finely. Put aside the outer shells, ready for stuffing.

Meanwhile, soften the mushrooms in tepid water for a few minutes. Drain the mushrooms, reserving the soaking liquid, and squeeze out and reserve any excess water.

Chop the mushrooms and fry them in the butter. Add a tablespoon of the water from the mushrooms and, after a few minutes, stir in the veal and sausagemeat. Sauté until the meat is cooked, about 10 minutes.

Pour the meat and mushrooms into a bowl and mix with the chopped onion flesh, the egg, a pinch of salt and pepper and a little nutmeg.

Place the onion shells in an oiled, deep, heavy-based flameproof casserole. Stuff them with the meat mixture. Pour a ladleful of hot water (you can use any remaining mushroom-soaking liquid) over the onions, cover and cook, sprinkling now and again with their own cooking juices, for 10 minutes.

FAGIOLINI ALLA FIORENTINA

FLORENTINE FRENCH BEANS

Serves 4

150g/5oz french (green) beans
90ml/3fl oz/scant ½ cup olive oil
1 onion, chopped
½ tsp ground fennel seeds
1 tbsp tomato purée (paste), diluted
   in a little tepid water
salt

Apart from potatoes, if you gave my father a tomato that was all he wanted in life. My mother used to make this dish for him often. You can serve it as a vegetable dish and if there are leftovers, chop the beans into little pieces, add more tomatoes and garlic, and use as a sauce for any kind of pasta.

Clean the beans and soak them in cold water for about 20 minutes or until you are ready to cook them. (This refreshes them and makes them more crunchy.) Drain them and cook them in boiling, salted water for 10 minutes. Drain.

Heat the oil in a flameproof casserole and brown the onion in its with the fennel seeds. Add the diluted tomato purée (paste) and simmer for 3–4 minutes.

Stir in the cooked, drained beans, season to taste, cover and cook for a further 15 minutes.

FAGIOLI ALLA FIORENTINA

FLORENTINE BEANS

This dish was made by a lady from Florence called Signora Guidotti who lived in the manor house of the village. She used to invite me to eat with her because she had a daughter my age. They had such a different way of cooking that I thought they must be foreign. The first time she made this I asked the name of it and this is what she called it.

Serves 4

1 kg/2lb/2 cups fresh cannellini beans or 450g/1lb/1 cup dried beans
2 garlic cloves, chopped
1 leek, white part only, chopped
350g/12oz ripe tomatoes, peeled, de-seeded and chopped
100g/4oz green (unsmoked, uncured) belly of pork or streaky bacon, chopped
salt and freshly ground black pepper

If using dried beans, soak them in water for 6–7 hours or overnight.

Preheat the oven to 200°C/400°F/Gas Mark 6. Drain the beans and put in an ovenproof casserole with the garlic, leek, tomatoes, the belly pork or bacon and salt and pepper and cover with fresh, cold water. Put the lid on and bake for at least 1½ hours.

Taste to see if ready and serve piping hot.

FAGIOLI ALL'UCCELLETTO

TUSCAN BEAN STEW

The Tuscans are the greatest hunters in the whole of Italy. In the past, when we used to cook little birds, or uccelletti, *we would generally season them with sage. Although this dish contains no* uccelletto, *it reminds us of this tradition because it has sage in it. This is the most famous of the hundreds of ways to cook beans.*

Serves 4

1kg/2lb/2 cups fresh or dried cannellini or borlotti beans, or 450g/1lb/1 cup dried beans
90ml/3fl oz/scant ½ cup olive oil
3 garlic cloves, crushed
fresh sage leaves
350g/12oz ripe tomatoes, peeled, de-seeded and puréed
salt and freshly ground black pepper

If using dried beans, soak them in water for 6–7 hours or overnight. Then drain and rinse them and cook them in plenty of boiling water until soft, about 1–1½ hours. Drain.

If using fresh beans, shell them, then boil in slightly salted water until ready, 25–30 minutes. Drain.

Heat the oil in a saucepan and add the garlic, a few sage leaves and a sprinkling of pepper. Fry until the garlic is golden, then add the cooked beans and the puréed tomatoes. Cook for 10 minutes.

Season with salt and pepper before serving.

CIME DI RAPE SALTATE

SAUTÉED TURNIP TOPS

Turnip tops resemble tiny broccoli. As a child, when I saw the shoots of the turnip tops come up, I was always happy for two reasons: because I knew how delicious they were, and because I knew spring was in the air! In England, when I go shooting, I always ask the farmer if I can have some of his turnip tops. Once, I gave them to him for dinner and he was astonished because they were so delicious. 'This shows how uncivilized we are,' he said. 'We usually just feed these to the animals!' This dish makes a very good accompaniment for pork and also as a sauce for short pasta shapes, such as fusilli or large macaroni.

Serves 4

500g/1lb 2oz turnip tops
2 tbsp olive oil
2 garlic cloves, finely chopped
salt and freshly ground black pepper

Wash the turnip tops, drain, then cook in just the water clinging to the leaves for 5 minutes or so, until softened. Drain.

Heat the oil in a frying-pan and brown the garlic. Stir in the turnip tops and cook for 5 minutes. Season to taste with salt and pepper.

STUFATO DI PISELLI

PEA CASSEROLE

This is a dish my sister makes very well. Even today she will be sure to cook it for me if I go to visit her in Italy. I can make it almost as well – but not quite – only if I use tiny petit pois. You can eat this with pasta – especially small, shell-shaped pasta.

Serves 4

90ml/3fl oz/scant ½ cup olive oil
1 onion, finely chopped
400g/14oz/1 cup shelled fresh peas
chicken or light meat stock
1 tsp sugar
salt and freshly ground black pepper

Put the oil in an earthenware or other heavy-based, flameproof casserole or heavy frying-pan (skillet) and gently fry the onion until translucent. Add the peas and stir thoroughly. Season and add a little hot stock. Cook for 15 minutes, adding more stock from time to time, should the mixture dry out.

Just before removing from the heat, add the sugar, season to taste with salt and pepper, stir and serve.

FAGIOLI AL FIASCO

FLASK-COOKED BEANS

This is a very famous dish which is to the Tuscans what the tea ceremony is to the Japanese. It was traditionally eaten on special feast days, especially All Saints Day in November, when the first dried food – such as figs and tomatoes – was tested out for the coming winter. The dry beans were steamed in a flask with very little water and with cotton wool placed in the neck, and the flask was left to cook slowly in the hot embers of the hearth overnight. Today you can use a pressure cooker.

Serves 4

1kg/2lb/2 cups fresh cannellini or borlotti beans,
   or 450g/1lb/1 cup dried beans
90ml/3fl oz/scant ½ cup olive oil
2 garlic cloves, crushed
fresh sage leaves

To serve:
best-quality extra-virgin olive oil
salt and freshly ground black pepper

Shell the beans and pour them into a traditional Italian wine flask, from which you have removed the straw covering. Add the oil, garlic, a few sage leaves and two ladlefuls of water.

Seal the flask mouth with a towel or cotton cloth to prevent the liquid from spilling out during cooking. Place the flask upright on tepid charcoal. Leave to cook for several hours. You can use a pressure cooker instead of a flask, in which case, cook the beans for 20 minutes. To cook in a lidded flameproof casserole, cook for 35 minutes.

When ready, pour into a bowl, dress with olive oil, salt and pepper and serve with toast.

FUNGHI ALLA TOSCANA

MUSHROOM CASSEROLE

In Italy, wild mushrooms grow abundantly. When we make this dish at home, we use many different kinds of wild mushroom: they have a far more intense flavour than the ordinary white ones you can buy. Nipitella – like a cross between mint and oregano – also grows wild. In fact there is so much of it around that farmers find they can't get rid of it! It used to grow around our house so I would pick it for my mother while she cooked. My family used to eat this as a main course, but now it is more often used as a side dish. As a variation to this recipe, you can substitute three eggs, beaten with a little lemon juice, for the tomato purée (paste); add the eggs to the mushrooms 2–3 minutes before removing from the heat.

Serves 4

500g/1lb 2oz fresh porcini mushrooms
3 garlic cloves
90ml/3fl oz/scant ½ cup olive oil
1 fresh nipitella (wild mint) or fresh garden mint sprig
1 tsp tomato purée (paste), diluted in a small amount of hot water
salt and freshly ground black pepper

Scrape the mushrooms clean with a knife and wash and dry them. Cut the stems off and thinly slice both stems and caps.

Place the garlic cloves in an earthenware or other heavy-based, flameproof casserole and brown in the oil with the mint sprig. Gently stir in the mushrooms and fry them for a few more minutes. Season to taste. Lower the heat and simmer, adding a little hot water if necessary, for 5 minutes or until the mushrooms are cooked.

Remove the garlic and mint and blend in the diluted tomato purée (paste); cook for a further 2–3 minutes.

CARCIOFI IN PIEDE ALLA FIORENTINA

FLORENTINE-STYLE ARTICHOKES

My family used to eat this on feast days, especially on 19 March, which is Saint Joseph's Day. It is normally served as a vegetable dish, but can also be a main course on its own.

Serves 4

8 medium-size globe artichokes
juice of ½ lemon
100g/4oz pancetta or streaky bacon, chopped
1 tbsp chopped fresh parsley
90ml/3fl oz/scant ½ cup olive oil
salt and freshly ground black pepper

Remove and discard all the hard outer leaves and the spiky tips of the artichokes, so you end up with a stalk, heart and three-quarters of the tender leaves. Peel the stalks until you get to the tender part and then soak the artichokes in cold water, to which you have added some lemon juice, for 30 minutes.

Drain the artichokes thoroughly and place them, tips upwards, so that they tightly fit into a flameproof casserole or heavy-based saucepan.

Sprinkle them with the chopped pancetta or bacon and parsley, season generously with salt and pepper and add oil and water in equal parts. You need enough to keep the artichokes moist but not immersed, so keep the pan about a quarter full.

Cover and simmer gently for 25 minutes, adding a little more water should the bottom of the saucepan dry out. Now and again, gather the gravy with a spoon and pour it over the artichokes for added flavour.

You can serve the cooked artichokes straight from the saucepan.

CARCIOFINI FRITTI

FRIED BABY ARTICHOKES

Artichokes are a vegetable we use a lot in Italy – the best ones to use are the smallest that come from the second picking. When my mother made these fritters we would either eat them hot or leave them on the table to eat during the day. They can be served as a starter and also as a vegetable dish, like Fiori Di Zucca Fritti (see page 56). You can also serve a mixture of the two dishes.

Serves 4

10 small artichokes
juice of 1 lemon
olive oil for deep-frying
plain (all-purpose) white flour for coating
2 eggs, beaten
salt and freshly ground black pepper

Remove and discard all the hard outer leaves of the artichokes and cut off the spiky tips, so you end up with a stalk, heart and three-quarters of the tender leaves. Slice into thin strips and soak in a basin of cold water, to which you have added the juice of a lemon to prevent them from discolouring.

After approximately 30 minutes, drain and dry thoroughly.

Heat the oil for deep-frying until it is very hot; a cube of day-old bread should brown in less than a minute.

Toss the artichoke slices in the flour and dip into the beaten eggs, which you have seasoned with salt and pepper. When they are well coated, deep-fry them until they are golden and crisp. Do this in batches if necessary, and reheat the oil between each batch. Drain the fritters on kitchen paper and keep them warm while you cook the rest. Serve as soon as possible.

FIORI DI ZUCCA FRITTI

DEEP-FRIED MARROW FLOWERS

We used to eat these all through the summer until the first frosts at the end of October. If possible, you should try to use the female plant which has no marrow – the flowers have a better flavour. They can be served as a starter and also as a vegetable dish, like Carciofini Fritti (see page 55). You can also serve a mixture of the two dishes.

Serves 6

18 vegetable marrow or courgette (zucchini) flowers
2 eggs
2 tbsp plain (all-purpose) white flour
olive oil for deep-frying
salt and freshly ground black pepper

Clean the flowers by removing any green leaves and the pistils, and then rinse and dry them carefully.

Beat the eggs in a basin with salt and pepper. Blend in the flour and enough water to make a thick batter.

Heat the oil for deep-frying until very hot; a cube of day-old bread should brown in less than a minute.

Dip the flowers in the batter and coat thoroughly. Fry them in the hot oil until golden. Do this in batches if necessary, and reheat the oil between each batch. Drain on kitchen paper and keep warm while you cook the rest. When all are ready, season and serve on a warmed platter.

BACCELLI STUFATI

STEWED BROAD (FAVA) BEANS

Around the beginning of May, when our garden began to give back all the hard work we had put into it during the winter and spring, broad (fava) beans were the first crop we would pick. We would eat this as a main course, but it is also very suitable as a side dish or as a pasta sauce: I recommend rigatoni.

Serves 4

100g/4oz pancetta or streaky bacon
2 garlic cloves, bruised
90ml/3fl oz/scant ½ cup olive oil
500g/1lb 2oz/1 cup fresh broad (fava) beans, shelled
vegetable or light chicken stock or hot water
chopped fresh parsley
salt and freshly ground black pepper

Fry the pancetta or bacon and garlic in the oil. Remove the garlic when golden. Add the broad (fava) beans and sauté for a few minutes. Then add salt, pepper, a little stock or hot water and the parsley.

Simmer until the beans are cooked, adding a little more stock or water if necessary.

CARCIOFI ALLA PAESANA

FARMHOUSE ARTICHOKES

This dish used to be made by a lady who lived near our house. She was called Arduina and came from the Apennines. I always knew when she was cooking this because I could smell its delicious aroma from a distance – she knew I liked it so she always gave me some. It can also be used as a pasta sauce, provided that thick pasta, such as macaroni, is used.

Serves 6

6 globe artichokes
juice of 1 lemon
90ml/3fl oz/scant ½ cup olive oil
3 garlic cloves
1 fresh nipitella (wild mint) or fresh garden mint sprig
1 tsp tomato purée (paste), diluted in a little tepid water
salt and freshly ground black pepper

Clean the artichokes. Remove and discard the hard outer leaves and the spiky tips, so you end up with a stalk, heart and three-quarters of the tender leaves. Wash them and cut into segments. Peel the stalks. Soak all the artichoke parts in water and lemon juice for 30 minutes. Drain and dry the artichoke segments.

Heat the oil in an earthenware or other heavy-based, flameproof casserole or heavy frying-pan (skillet). Fry the garlic and the mint sprig. When the garlic is golden, remove it and add the artichoke pieces. Stir for a few minutes, season to taste and add the diluted tomato purée (paste).

Cook for 5 minutes and then add a ladleful of hot water and continue cooking until the artichokes are tender, about 15–20 minutes, adding a little more hot water if necessary to prevent them from drying out.

SEDANI ALLA CONTADINA

FARMHOUSE CELERY

Serves 8

2 heads of celery
plain (all-purpose) white flour for coating
2 eggs, beaten
fresh white breadcrumbs for coating
olive oil for deep-frying
25g/1oz/¼ cup grated parmesan cheese

For the meat sauce:
200g/7oz chicken livers
175ml/6fl oz/¼ cup olive oil
1 onion, finely chopped
100g/4oz prosciutto crudo (raw cured ham),
   finely minced (ground) in the food processor
200g/7oz minced (ground) veal
90ml/3fl oz/scant ½ cup dry white wine
salt, pepper and grated nutmeg
25g/1oz/¼ cup grated parmesan cheese

Contadina *means a farm worker or peasant – someone who could not afford meat or, if they could, it would not be the best cut. A dish like this would be a way of stretching the meat by using lots of different ingredients. Italians don't tend to eat celery raw, and if you try to sell celery without any leaves, they will think you are a mad person. This is because the leaves are often used as a flavouring for soups – indeed, it is probably the most common herb used in this way.*

Clean the celery, removing and discarding the toughest parts and the hardest leaves and separating the sticks; then wash and boil them in plenty of salted water for 10 minutes.

To make the meat sauce
Trim, wash and chop the chicken livers.

Place the oil in a casserole and fry the onion until softened. Add the ham and, when it is well browned, add the veal. Fry for a few more minutes and then stir in the chicken livers. Pour in the wine and season with salt, pepper and nutmeg. Cook for about 25 minutes.

When cooked, remove from the heat and sprinkle with the parmesan; return to the heat, just to melt the parmesan.

To cook the celery
Drain the celery and cut each stick to a length of about 7–8cm/3–3½ inches. Open up the sticks, pressing down on them with the palm of your hand. Stuff each celery stick with some of the meat and liver mixture, and then press back the edges. Coat each stick in flour and then dip into the beaten eggs; season the celery sticks and toss them in the breadcrumbs.

Heat the oil for deep-frying until very hot; a cube of day-old bread should brown in less than a minute.

Fry the celery sticks until golden, about 4 minutes. Do this in batches if necessary, reheating the oil between batches. Remove the celery with a slotted spoon and then place in a greased ovenproof dish in layers of celery, parmesan and meat sauce. Bake in a hot oven for 15 minutes, or until the surface is a beautiful golden brown colour.

PASTA

I LOVE TO MAKE PASTA. WHENEVER I MAKE IT, NO MATTER WHAT DAY OF THE WEEK IT IS, I ALWAYS THINK IT IS A SUNDAY OR A FEAST DAY OF SOME SORT. WHEN MY MOTHER MADE PASTA, SHE WOULD LET ME HELP, SO MAKING FRESH PASTA WAS THE FIRST CONTACT I EVER HAD WITH COOKING. ONE OF MY EARLIEST RECOLLECTIONS IS WHEN I WAS SIX – IT WAS THE THIRD OF JUNE, MY BIRTHDAY – AND I WAS IN CHARGE OF PUSHING THE HANDLE ON THE PASTA-ROLLING MACHINE. THIS SHOWS YOU HOW SOFT PASTA MUST BE, IF A CHILD OF SIX CAN DO THIS! WHEN IT GOES INTO THE MACHINE, IT SOUNDS LIKE IT'S KISSING YOU BECAUSE IT MAKES A SOFT POPPING NOISE. TODAY, EVERYBODY IS ALWAYS AMAZED WHEN I MAKE PASTA BECAUSE I DO IT SO FAST!

There have always been arguments about how pasta arrived in the Mediterranean and when it became the staple food throughout much of Italy.

Some say that pasta arrived from China; others have discovered that pasta was being eaten many centuries before Christ and attribute this to the Etruscans. There has also been speculation that pasta arrived as late as the medieval period.

There is proof that the Etruscans discovered pasta, as they were already cooking 'laganae' (lasagne). Clay dishes have been found as a testament to their civilization. The name macaroni may date back to ancient Rome; it derives from the Latin *maccare*, which means 'to knead'.

There are also records that, at the time of the Moorish invasion in the thirteenth century in Sicily, dried pasta was being made commercially. The various shapes have not yet been defined.

Marco Polo found in China a food similar to lasagne. In 1492, the famous Italian historian Platino, who researched the origins of food, wrote *Dicta vermicelli*, in which he described the shape of pasta as like 'little worms', which was taken up into common parlance. Around the same time, in Florence, there were single Sicilian women who opened workshops in which they made pasta.

In the middle of the 1500s, pasta was being made in Liguria, Lazio and Campania. The dough was kneaded with the feet, as this new cult, *pasta*, was considered sacred and its making was treated as a ritual.

Whatever its origin, the art of pasta, the Italian spaghetti and macaroni which we love so much, certainly reached great heights in the Renaissance. In the 1500s, there were many artisans making pasta as we know it today. In the 1600s, pasta was being consumed in great quantities. By the middle of the

1700s, in Naples, machinery took over and pasta-making became more resourceful, making pasta not only a cheap and nourishing food in the poor, over-populated areas of the Mediterranean, but also an industry.

From the Alps right down to the island of Sicily, pasta is consumed on a daily basis. Each region of Italy has its own speciality, making pasta a national tradition and a habit without which mealtimes just become snacks.

A Note on Making Pasta

The best flour to use for making pasta is Italian '00' flour or an 'extra-strong' white flour suitable for bread-making.

To make pasta, you need about 100g/4oz/generous 1/2 cup of flour, 1 egg, 1 tbsp olive oil and a pinch of salt per person. Pile the flour on to a work surface. Make a hole in the centre and put the eggs, olive oil and salt into the hollow. Mix the eggs and oil into the flour and knead until you have a firm, smooth, elastic dough. You need to achieve a soft texture (like a lady's cheek), so the exact quantity of flour will depend on the size of the eggs. Knead the pasta until it feels soft and smooth, then pass it at least 10 times through a hand-cranked pasta-rolling machine, if you have one. It is very difficult to roll it by hand thinly enough to make lasagne or pappardelle, unless you are very experienced.

At home, you can really only make egg pasta successfully; otherwise, it is much better to buy a good-quality brand of dry pasta.

FUSILLI CON POMODORI SECCHI

PASTA TWISTS WITH SUN-DRIED

TOMATOES

Serves 4

800g/1lb 12oz fusilli (pasta twists)
250ml/8fl oz/1 cup good olive oil
125g/4½ oz/1½ cups pine nuts
125g/4oz sun-dried tomatoes, sliced
100g/4oz/1 cup grated parmesan cheese
350g/12oz pecorino cheese, diced
3–4 large fresh basil sprigs, chopped
salt and freshly ground black pepper

This is a summery dish which is also very Mediterranean. It is something that my mother used to make if she had very little time because it is very easy to prepare. Sun-dried tomatoes are not a new thing at all – in fact, this recipe dates back to the Arab invasion of Sicily in the ninth century. I first used them in one of my restaurants in 1966. Serve this dish either hot or cold but, if you are serving it hot, you need to serve it immediately.

Cook the pasta as normal, in a large pan in lots of salted, boiling water, until *al dente* or tender but still with a slight 'bite'.

Meanwhile, heat 1 tbsp of the oil in a frying-pan (skillet) and lightly brown the pine nuts. To serve hot, drain the pasta and toss it with all the other ingredients.

To serve cold, refresh the pasta under cold water in a colander, then toss the cold pasta with the other ingredients.

PASTA D'ESTATE

SUMMER PASTA SALAD

A little more sophisticated than the previous recipe, this can be eaten either hot or cold. To me, it is better hot. I remember eating it in front of our house under the fig tree that grew there – my mother would place a huge bowl in the middle of the table and everyone would help themselves.

I have used pasta bows, but you can make it with any kind of short pasta. A tip: whenever you have a heavy sauce, use rather thick pasta; for a more delicate sauce, use more delicate pasta. A heavy pasta will overpower a delicate sauce and vice versa.

Serves 6

800g/1lb 12oz farfalle (pasta bows)
150ml/¼ pint/⅔ cup good olive oil
60ml/4 tbsp white-wine vinegar
1 tbsp wholegrain mustard
150g/5oz/1¾ cups pine nuts, toasted
350g/12oz cherry tomatoes, halved
275g/10oz baby spinach leaves
125g/4½ oz/generous 1 cup grated parmesan cheese
salt and freshly ground black pepper

Cook the pasta as normal, in a large pan in lots of salted, boiling water, until *al dente* or tender but still with a slight 'bite'.

Meanwhile, whisk together the oil, vinegar and mustard as a dressing and set it aside.

Drain the pasta, refresh with cold water and place in a large serving bowl. Toss together the pasta, dressing and all the remaining ingredients.

PAPPARDELLE CON LA LEPRE

PASTA WITH HARE SAUCE

Serves 6

1 medium-sized hare, weighing about
   2.7–3.6kg/6–8lb
500ml/17fl oz/2¼ cups robust red wine
1 carrot, chopped
1 onion, sliced
1 celery stick, chopped
bouquet garni of fresh parsley, thyme and
   rosemary sprigs
1 tbsp mixed juniper berries and black
   peppercorns
2 tbsp olive oil
salt
butter
grated parmesan cheese, to serve

For the pasta:
500g/1lb 2oz/3 cups strong white flour
5 eggs, beaten
1 tbsp olive oil
1 tsp salt

You can find this dish all over Tuscany. When you mention the word pappardelle, you are actually saying Tuscany. Pappardelle is a ribbon-shaped pasta which is served with lots of different sauces, but always heavy ones. A hare sauce such as this is only eaten in November during the hunting season – you could also use bolognese, mutton (as you will see in the recipe for Pappardelle Al Sugo Di Pecora, see page 68) or duck.

Clean and wash the hare. Cut it into joints and leave to drain.

Place the joints in an earthenware or other heavy-based, flameproof casserole and marinate them in the wine with the carrot, onion, celery, bouquet garni, juniper berries and peppercorns for 4–5 hours. Turn the pieces over occasionally, to ensure that they all get well coated in the marinade.

Meanwhile, make the pasta in the normal way (see page 62). Roll it out through a pasta-rolling machine, not too thinly (it should be about 1–1.5mm thick). Cut it into strips 2cm/³⁄₄ inch wide and lay them on a floured cloth.

Remove the meat, strain the marinade and reserve it. Heat the olive oil in the casserole, add the meat and brown it all over; season with salt. Keep adding tablespoons of marinade to prevent the hare from drying out.

When the hare is cooked, about 20 minutes, take out the saddle and leg pieces, remove any bones and mince (grind) the meat. Strain the sauce, discarding any other pieces of hare, and cook it in a clean saucepan, with the minced (ground) meat and a knob of butter, for about 10 minutes, stirring frequently.

Cook the pasta in a large pan in lots of salted, boiling water until *al dente* or tender but still with a slight 'bite'. Drain and arrange on a platter in layers with the hare sauce and some grated parmesan.

PAPPARDELLE AL SUGO DI PECORA

PASTA RIBBONS WITH LAMB SAUCE

Serves 6

2 tbsp olive oil
1 onion, finely chopped
1 carrot, finely chopped
1 celery stick, finely chopped
bouquet garni of 1 fresh rosemary sprig and
    1 fresh thyme sprig
500g/1lb 2oz very lean lamb or mutton
    (breast, leg or loin), cut in small cubes
175ml/6fl oz/³⁄₄ cup dry white wine
500g/1lb 2oz ripe tomatoes, skinned,
    de-seeded and puréed
chicken or light meat stock
salt and freshly ground black pepper
butter and grated parmesan cheese, to serve

For the pasta:
500g/1lb 2oz/3 cups strong white flour
5 eggs, beaten
1 tbsp olive oil
1 tsp salt

Lamb is eaten very seldom in Italy. This dish, which is a little like a bolognese sauce, but made with lamb, comes from Pistoia, a province of northern Tuscany. People come from all over Italy to eat the lamb here. This is another quite heavy sauce of the type that is usually served with pappardelle.

Heat the olive oil in an earthenware or other heavy-based, flame-proof casserole, and sauté the onion, carrot and celery with the bouquet garni.

Add the meat and, when it is well browned, sprinkle with salt and pepper and pour in the wine, raising the heat to evaporate the alcohol. Then stir in the tomatoes and cook, adding a little hot stock if necessary, for 30 minutes.

Meanwhile, make the pasta in the normal way (see page 62). Roll it out through a pasta-rolling machine, not too thinly (it should be about 1–1.5mm thick). Cut it into strips 2cm/³⁄₄ inch wide and lay them on a floured cloth.

Bring a large pan of salted water to the boil. Slide the pasta strips into the boiling water and cook until *al dente* or tender but still with a slight 'bite'. Drain the pasta and arrange a layer on a warmed platter. Dress with the meat sauce, keeping as many of the largest pieces of meat back as possible; dot with butter and sprinkle with grated parmesan cheese. Repeat the layers until all the ingredients are used up. Garnish the top layer with the reserved meat cubes and serve immediately.

FETTUCCINE ALL'ANATRA

PASTA RIBBONS WITH DUCK SAUCE

Serves 6

1.2kg/2½ lb duck, with its liver
3 tbsp olive oil
100g/4oz prosciutto crudo (raw cured ham), diced
1 onion, chopped
1 carrot, chopped
1 celery stick, chopped
2 fresh sage leaves
90ml/3fl oz/scant ½ cup dry white wine
500g/1lb 2oz tomatoes, skinned, de-seeded and puréed
chicken or light meat stock
salt and freshly ground black pepper
butter and grated parmesan cheese, to serve

For the pasta:
500g/1lb 2oz/3 cups strong white flour
5 eggs, beaten
1 tbsp olive oil
1 tsp salt

This is probably the second best-known recipe in Tuscany. I remember that we used to eat it at the end of the grape harvest, when there were lots of students around helping us, and we had a special dinner to celebrate. It's important to use duck liver; if you can only buy a duck without giblets, buy extra livers separately. You can use chicken livers, but the flavour won't be so good: soak them in water for about half an hour before chopping.

Clean the duck. Remove the liver, chop it and set aside. Wash the duck inside and out and cut it into pieces. Leave to drain thoroughly.

Heat the oil in an earthenware or other flameproof, heavy-based casserole and seal the pieces of duck all over, with the ham, the onion, carrot, celery and sage. When the meat is well browned, sprinkle with salt and pepper and pour in the wine. Cook until the alcohol has evaporated.

Add the tomatoes and leave to cook for 1 hour, adding spoonfuls of hot stock as necessary, to prevent the sauce from drying out. After approximately 45 minutes, stir in the duck liver.

Meanwhile, make the pasta in the normal way (see page 62). Roll it out, not too thinly, and cut into strips 4mm/¹⁄₂ inch wide. Place the strips on a floured cloth. Cook the pasta in a large pan of boiling, salted water until *al dente* or tender but still with a slight 'bite'.

Remove the pieces of duck and the liver from the gravy and strain the gravy.

When the pappardelle are done, drain and arrange them in layers on a warmed platter, alternating them with the strained duck gravy, together with the liver, knobs of butter and grated parmesan. Serve the pieces of duck on the side.

PASTASCIUTTA ALLA FORNAIA

THE BAKER'S PASTA

This sauce is very much like pesto but with more emphasis on the walnuts and the pecorino. The recipe was given to me by my cousin who has a restaurant in Tuscany called Rosticceria Nardini.

Serves 6

75g/3oz fresh basil leaves
50g/2oz walnut kernels
100g/4oz aged pecorino cheese
175ml/6fl oz/¾ cup olive oil
500g/1lb 2oz long pasta, e.g. spaghetti or tagliatelle
salt and freshly ground black pepper

Grind the basil, walnuts and pecorino with a pestle and mortar. Season with salt and pepper. When you have a well blended paste, trickle in the olive oil, stirring it in with a wooden spoon. You can make the pesto in a food processor if you prefer, but you will need to add more oil and drain off the excess.

Bring a large pan of salted water to the boil. Add the pasta and cook until *al dente* or tender but still with a slight 'bite'. Drain and serve dressed with the basil sauce.

PASTA ALLA CONTADINA

PEASANT-STYLE PASTA

This is a very colourful sauce. We used to have this during the week – a good basic meal.

Serves 4

250g/9oz fresh button mushrooms, sliced thinly
3 tbsp olive oil
1 onion, chopped
1 tsp chopped fresh parsley, plus extra to serve
300g/11oz tomatoes, skinned, de-seeded and puréed
500g/1lb 2oz linguine or other long pasta, e.g spaghetti or tagliatelle
salt and freshly ground black pepper
grated pecorino and parmesan cheese, to serve

Clean the mushrooms by scraping them with a small knife. Wash, dry and cut them into thin slices.

In an earthenware or other heavy-based, flameproof casserole, heat the oil and fry the onion and parsley until softened. Add the mushrooms and cook for a few more minutes. Then stir in the tomatoes, season with salt and pepper and simmer over a low heat for about 40 minutes.

Bring a large pan of salted water to the boil and cook the pasta until *al dente* or tender but still with a slight 'bite'. Drain and toss with the mushroom sauce. Sprinkle with parsley and generous helpings of pecorino and parmesan cheese and serve.

GNOCCHI DI SPINACI AL FORNO

OVEN-BAKED GNOCCHI

Serves 4

For the gnocchi:
500g/1lb 2oz fresh spinach
500ml/17fl oz/2¼ cups milk
1 tbsp butter
200g/7oz semolina
2 eggs, beaten
50g/2oz/½ cup grated parmesan cheese
salt

For the white sauce:
40g/1½ oz/2 tbsp butter
2 tbsp plain (all-purpose) white flour
500ml/17fl oz/2¼ cups milk
salt and grated nutmeg
50g/2oz/½ cup grated parmesan cheese

Gnocchi are a very popular dish, either green (made with spinach) as in this recipe, or yellow (made with polenta) as in the recipe for Gnocchi Di Farina Gialla (see page 74). This dish is typically served on a Sunday because it can be kept warm in the oven, with sauce and cheese on top, for as long as you want – you can talk and drink and the dinner will not be ruined.

Preheat the oven to 220°C/425°F/Gas Mark 7.

To make the gnocchi
Wash the spinach, then cook in the water clinging to the leaves. Let the spinach cool and then squeeze it dry in your hands. Finely chop it by hand or in a food processor.

Bring the milk to the boil. Melt the butter into it and then rain the semolina into the boiling milk a little at a time, stirring constantly to prevent lumps from forming. Cook over a low heat for around 10 minutes.

Remove from the heat and blend in the spinach, the beaten eggs, the parmesan and a pinch of salt, stirring vigorously.

To prepare the white sauce
Melt the butter in a saucepan and add the flour, stirring energetically to a smooth paste. Stir in the milk and continue to cook, stirring all the time, until the sauce has thickened. Season with salt and nutmeg and add the parmesan.

Shape the gnocchi mixture into small pieces, place them in a buttered ovenproof dish and cover them with the white sauce. Bake for 20–25 minutes.

GNUDI

NAKED GNOCCHI

So-called because this is the filling of ravioli, with no pasta casing at all! This is very popular with people on a diet or those who think that pasta is fattening. I used to help my mother to prepare these gnocchi by rolling a teaspoonful of the mixture around inside a glass to make them round.

Serves 4

300g/11oz fresh spinach
300g/11oz ricotta cheese, crumbled
50g/2oz/½ cup grated parmesan or pecorino cheese
3 eggs
plain (all-purpose) white flour
salt, pepper and grated nutmeg
chicken or light meat stock for cooking (optional)

To serve:
Ragu di Carne alla Pistoiese (page 178), bolognese sauce or melted butter and grated parmesan cheese

Wash the spinach, then cook in the water clinging to the leaves after washing. Drain and squeeze it dry, and then chop very finely.

In a bowl, mix the crumbled ricotta, the spinach, the parmesan or pecorino and the eggs. Season with salt, pepper and nutmeg. Work in enough flour to make a fairly compact mixture, the consistency of potato purée.

Shape into lumps the size of a walnut and place on a floured cloth.

Cook the gnocchi for a few minutes in either boiling water or stock. Serve them in the stock or, if you have cooked them in water, drain and dress with either a meat sauce, or melted butter and grated parmesan cheese.

GNOCCHI DI FARINA GIALLA

POLENTA GNOCCHI

My grandmother used to make these after the first harvest on the first cold October day of the year. It was actually a way of testing the flour to see if it was good enough to make polenta for the whole winter.

Serves 4

600g/1lb 5oz /4 cups fairly coarse polenta
50g/2oz/¼ cup butter
75g/3oz/generous ½ cup grated parmesan cheese
salt

To serve:
Ragu di Carne alla Pistoiese (page 178), bolognese sauce or melted butter and grated parmesan cheese

Bring 2 litres/3½ pints/8⅔ cups of salted water to the boil. Trickle in the polenta like rain and cook, stirring frequently to prevent lumps from forming.

When the polenta is fairly soft, add the butter and 30g/1oz of parmesan. Remove from the heat.

Using a knife and spoon (which you will have to keep dipping in cold water), spoon oval-shaped lumps of the polenta on to a warmed platter. Arrange in layers, each sprinkled with parmesan, alternating polenta gnocchi and meat sauce.

TORTELLI DI PATATE

POTATO DUMPLINGS

Serves 4

For the pasta:
350g/12oz/2½ cups strong white flour
½ tsp salt
3 eggs, beaten

For the filling:
750g/1½lb white potatoes
75g/3oz/¾ cup grated parmesan cheese
30g/1oz/2 tbsp butter, softened
1 egg
salt and grated nutmeg

To serve:
Ragu di Carne alla Pistoiese (page 178) or
   bolognese sauce

When you make this recipe, it's like walking on stage! The most beautiful moment is when you put the dumplings into the boiling water and wait for them to come up – only then do you know that they are ready. I've made these dumplings for 40 years, and I'm still worried that one day they won't come up! My family used to eat this dish mainly in the cold winter months. I can still remember watching the potatoes steaming on the table and misting up the windows of the kitchen. Sometimes we call this 'Poor Man's Ravioli', because the only filling ingredients are cheese and potato.

To make the pasta
Pour the flour like a light rain on to the work surface, sprinkle with salt, make a hollow in the middle with your fist and add the eggs. Knead the ingredients together until you have a smooth and elastic dough, cover with a clean teatowel and set aside while you prepare the filling.

To make the filling
Boil the potatoes whole in plenty of salted water. When they are cooked, peel them and push them through a sieve, potato ricer or mouli. Beat in two-thirds of the parmesan, the butter, the egg, a pinch of salt and a generous pinch of nutmeg.

Knead the pasta dough again and roll it out into a thin sheet, about 1.5mm thick. On half of the dough, place small lumps of filling, leaving about 3 cm/1¼ inches between the lumps. Cover with the other half of the dough and press down with your fingers around each lump. Cut into squares with a pastry cutter and arrange on a floured cloth until you are ready to cook them.

Slide the tortelli into a saucepan of salted, boiling water and drain after a few minutes. Place on a warmed platter and serve with the pistoiese or bolognese meat sauce and the remaining grated parmesan.

PENNE CON PROSCIUTTO E ASPARAGI

PENNE WITH ASPARAGUS AND PROSCIUTTO

Serves 6

800g/1lb 12 oz penne (pasta quills)
30g/1oz/2 tbsp butter
450g/1lb asparagus spears or tiny broccoli
   florets (or a combination of both), blanched
4 tbsp chopped fresh parsley
225g/8oz Parma ham, sliced
125g/4oz/generous 1 cup grated parmesan
   cheese
salt and freshly ground black pepper

This is a dish that my Aunt Dailia used to make. She lived in a village where everyone from the surrounding area would gather to celebrate the first of May – and this is what she would cook on that day. As most people did at that time, she grew her own asparagus and produced her own prosciutto.

Cook the pasta as normal, in a large pan in lots of salted, boiling water, until *al dente* or tender but still with a slight 'bite'.

Just before the pasta is ready, melt the butter in a large frying-pan (skillet) and lightly sauté the asparagus and/or broccoli.

Drain the pasta and toss it with the vegetables.

Stir well, and then toss in the remaining ingredients, gently heat through and serve immediately.

TAGLIATELLE AL SUGO DI PROSCIUTTO

NOODLES WITH HAM SAUCE

This recipe was given to me by a friend who owns a restaurant called Le Panche in the Tuscan hills. I thought it was so nice, I decided to include it in my book.

Serves 4

For the pasta:
300g/11oz/2 cups strong white flour
1 tsp salt
1 tsp olive oil
3 eggs, beaten

For the sauce:
150g/5oz prosciutto crudo (raw cured ham), finely chopped
olive oil, if necessary
1 onion, finely chopped
1 small carrot, finely chopped
500g/1lb 2oz ripe tomatoes or 2 x 400g/14oz cans tomatoes, drained
salt and freshly ground black pepper
50g/2oz/½ cup grated parmesan cheese, to serve

To make the pasta
Pile the flour on to a work surface, make a well in the centre, sprinkle with salt, add the olive oil and blend in the eggs. Knead the dough until it is smooth and elastic (add a little tepid water, if necessary, to make the correct, soft consistency, as there are fewer eggs in this pasta recipe than in others in this book).

Roll out the dough into a thin sheet, about 1–1.5mm thick, and cut it into strips 5mm/¼ inch wide. Alternatively, you can use a pasta-rolling machine. Place the strips on a floured cloth and let them stand while you make the sauce.

To make the sauce
Sauté the ham in a little oil, if necessary, and then add the onion and carrot. When the onion is translucent, push the tomatoes through a sieve into the pan. Season with salt and pepper and simmer for 15 minutes.

Meanwhile, cook the pasta in a large pan of salted, boiling water until *al dente* or tender but still with a slight 'bite'. Drain.

Arrange layers of pasta, sauce and grated parmesan on a warmed platter and serve at once.

LASAGNE DI MAGRO

BAKED VEGETABLE LASAGNE

Serves 6

For the lasagne:
500g/1lb 2oz/3 cups strong white flour
6 large eggs
salt
1 tsp olive oil

For the filling:
2 courgettes (zucchini)
2 carrots
100ml/4fl oz/½ cup olive oil
1 large onion, finely sliced
100g/4oz shelled peas
1 litre/1¾ pints/4⅓ cups Salsa Bianca (see page 176)
100g/4oz mushrooms, sliced
300g/11oz parmesan cheese, grated
100g/4oz tomatoes, skinned
150g/5oz mozzarella cheese, sliced

This is a very well-known Tuscan recipe, which dates back to the Etruscans, when meat was not used to make lasagne. It really is a Sunday dish – there's no two ways about it. This particular recipe comes from a cousin of mine who is a vegetarian. It's so good that if I go to visit her, I will always ask her to make it for me. If you don't want to make your own lasagne, use 500g/1lb 2oz of good-quality commercial dried lasagne.

Preheat the oven to 200°C/400°F/Gas Mark 6.

If using dried lasagne, cook the sheets until they are *al dente*.

If making your own lasagne, make the pasta in the usual way (see page 62) and roll it out to about 1–1.5mm thick. Cut it to make sheets of a suitable size for your baking dish.

Chop the courgettes (zucchini) and carrots into cubes of about 2cm/¾ inch.

Heat the olive oil in a large saucepan. Add the onion and fry until translucent and soft, then mix in the other vegetables. Cook for about 10 minutes, stirring continuously (do not cover the saucepan). They should be cooked but still *al dente*.

Pour 250ml/8fl oz/1 cup of béchamel sauce into an oiled baking dish (10 × 30 × 30cm/4 × 12 × 12 inch). Lay the lasagne in the baking dish, making sure that the sheets of lasagne do not overlap. Cover the first layer with a ladleful of vegetables, follow with a ladleful of white sauce, a fistful of raw sliced mushrooms, 2 tbsp parmesan cheese and a fistful of chopped tomatoes. Place another layer of lasagne on top and repeat until all the ingredients are used. Finally, arrange slices of mozzarella cheese on the top and bake for 25 minutes.

After you have taken it out of the oven, leave the lasagne for 10 minutes before serving.

POULTRY AND GAME

GOING BACK IN HISTORY, YOU WILL FIND THAT CHICKEN WAS CONSIDERED A LUXURIOUS COMMODITY, ONLY FOR THE RICH. ONE OF THE DISHES GIVEN HERE IS POLLO FRITTO (SEE PAGE 86), AND THIS RECIPE DATES BACK TO AROUND 1000AD. THIS DISH WAS NOT THEN QUITE HOW WE KNOW IT NOW: IT WAS THE SERVANTS' FOOD.THE CHICKEN WAS BONED AND THE BREAST AND LEG WENT TO THE LORD OF THE HOUSE; THE CARCASSES WERE CHOPPED INTO LITTLE PIECES, AND DIPPED IN BATTER. THERE ARE SEVERAL GAME DISHES AND GAME SAUCES IN THIS COLLECTION: THE TOSCANI (TUSCAN PEOPLE) ARE FAMOUS GAME HUNTERS. UNFORTUNATELY, THIS INCLUDES HUNTING SONGBIRDS AND THAT IS WHY IT IS VERY RARE TO HEAR A BIRD SINGING IN TUSCANY. I FEEL I HAVE TO TELL YOU BOTH THE GOOD AND THE BAD THINGS ABOUT TUSCANY! WHEN I WAS A CHILD WE USED TO HAVE CHICKEN QUITE OFTEN BECAUSE WE REARED THEM ON THE FARM WHERE I LIVED. MY MOTHER WOULD OFTEN COOK IT FOR US ON A SUNDAY, WHICH WAS TRADITIONALLY A DAY TO EAT MEAT.

POLLO AL LIMONE

CHICKEN WITH LEMON SAUCE

This lovely, delicate recipe was given to me by my sister. It is delicious served with a fresh green salad.

Serves 4

1.2kg/2lb 8oz chicken
30g/1oz/2 tbsp butter
2 tbsp chopped fresh parsley
1 lemon, cut in segments
90ml/3fl oz/scant ½ cup olive oil
3 garlic cloves, crushed
hot chicken stock
juice of 2 lemons
salt and freshly ground black pepper

Dry the chicken with kitchen paper and butter the inside of it as thoroughly as possible. Season the inside with salt and pepper and add 1 tbsp of parsley and a few lemon segments.

Put the oil in a deep saucepan and fry the garlic cloves and the remaining parsley until golden brown; then add the chicken and cook until browned all over. Season generously with salt and pepper. Cover the pan and cook for about 35 minutes, adding some hot stock now and again to prevent it from drying out. Test that the chicken is cooked by piercing the thickest part of the thigh with a skewer; the juices should run clear.

Pour the lemon juice over the chicken and cook for a further 5 minutes. Remove the chicken from the cooking liquid and cut it into joints. Reduce the cooking liquid to your desired thickness by rapid boiling, if necessary, and serve as a sauce.

POLLO ALLA BARONTANA

CHICKEN BARONTANA

Serves 4

1.2kg/2lb 8oz chicken
90ml/3fl oz/scant ½ cup olive oil
1 onion, sliced
175ml/6fl oz/¾ cup dry white wine
4 garlic cloves, chopped
leaves of 2 fresh rosemary sprigs, chopped
150g/5oz black olives
1 tbsp red-wine vinegar

There is a tiny village in the hills between Florence and Lucca called St Baronto, the only village in the world with this name. It is such a tiny village but most of the famous chefs of Tuscany were born here. This is why I have dedicated this dish to the village.

Cut the chicken into joints and pat them dry with kitchen paper. Put the oil in a deep saucepan and sauté the onion until browned; then add the chicken joints and cook until browned all over. Pour in the wine, cover and simmer until the chicken is cooked, about 25 minutes. Test by piercing the thigh with a skewer; the juices should run clear.

Add the garlic and rosemary, together with the olives and vinegar. Stir well and cook for 5 minutes more. Remove from the heat and serve.

POLLO FRITTO

FRIED CHICKEN

The Tuscans love to fry things, as good olive oil is so readily available. This is one of the oldest recipes known to Tuscany – it can be traced back to 1000AD and is still very common. Serve these crisp, tender chicken joints in batter on a platter, with chips, fried cardoons or fresh salad.

Serves 4

1.2kg/2lb 8oz chicken
2 eggs
salt
2 tbsp plain (all-purpose) white flour, sifted
olive oil for deep-frying

Cut the chicken into joints and dry the pieces with kitchen paper.

Beat the eggs with a pinch of salt in a bowl and then slowly blend in the flour, a tablespoon of oil and enough water to obtain a runny batter.

Heat the oil for deep-frying until it is very hot; a cube of day-old bread should brown in less than a minute.

Dip the chicken pieces into the batter and then fry them – in batches if necessary to avoid crowding the pan and lowering the oil temperature – until golden brown all over. This will take 8–10 minutes, depending on the size of the chicken and the temperature of the oil.

Drain on kitchen paper and keep warm while you deep-fry the remaining pieces; then serve at once.

POLLO ALLA DIAVOLA

CHICKEN WITH DEVILLED SAUCE

This recipe uses chilli peppers and is hot like the inferno – this is why we call it 'alla Diavola'. Serve with fresh salad.

Serves 4

1.2kg/2lb 8oz chicken
90ml/3fl oz/scant ½ cup olive oil
juice of 1 lemon
1 dried red chilli pepper, crushed in a mortar
salt and freshly ground black pepper
1 lemon, cut into segments, to serve

Dry the chicken well. Using a heavy knife, cut it along the backbone, open it and lightly beat it with a mallet, to flatten it.

In a bowl large enough to hold the chicken, prepare a marinade of olive oil mixed with the lemon juice, the crushed chilli pepper and salt and pepper. Put the chicken in the bowl and leave to marinate for half an hour. Turn it over and leave to marinate for another half hour.

Preheat the grill or barbecue or a wood fire. Thread two long metal skewers diagonally through the chicken, to hold it completely flat.

Grill for around 40 minutes. Check that the chicken is cooked by piercing the thickest part of the thigh with a skewer; the juices should run clear.

Serve hot, with lemon segments to squeeze over.

POLLO ALLA FIORENTINA

FLORENTINE CHICKEN

Rosemary was the herb we used in my family more than any other. When I asked my father why everything was made with rosemary, he told me that the Romans used to put rosemary over the bodies of the dead, so as the chicken is dead, we must also use rosemary. He was teasing me, of course! Serve with seasonal salad.

Serves 4

1.2kg/2lb 8oz chicken
175ml/6fl oz/¾ cup olive oil
juice of 1 lemon
1 fresh rosemary sprig
1 tsp chopped fresh parsley
2 bay leaves
salt and freshly ground black pepper

Dry the chicken well. Using a heavy knife, cut it along the backbone, open it and lightly beat it with a mallet, to flatten it.

In a bowl large enough to hold the chicken, prepare a marinade by mixing together the olive oil, lemon juice, herbs, salt and pepper. Put the chicken in the marinade and leave for 2 hours, turning it over a few times.

Preheat the grill or barbecue or a wood fire. Thread two long metal skewers diagonally through the chicken, to hold it flat.

Grill for around 30 minutes or until the chicken is golden on both sides. Check that the chicken is cooked by piercing the thickest part of the thigh with a skewer; the juices should run clear. Serve hot.

POLLO FARCITO

STUFFED CHICKEN

My mother used to cook chicken for us on a Sunday. As we grew accustomed to having chicken regularly, she had to embellish on the presentation of this dish, so she would stuff it in the way that you might stuff a chicken on Christmas Day. Nowadays, when I have this dish, I still have a sense of festivity. The number of servings depends on how hungry the diners are. A 1.5kg/3lb chicken can serve four hungry people or can be stretched to serve six. Serve with seasonal salad.

Serves 4

1.2–1.5kg/2–3lb chicken
1 onion, sliced
1 celery stick, sliced
1 carrot, sliced

For the stuffing:
300g/11oz swiss chard
150g/5oz fresh ricotta cheese
50g/2oz/½ cup grated parmesan cheese
2 tbsp fresh white breadcrumbs
pinch each of chopped fresh marjoram, basil, parsley and thyme
1 egg
salt, pepper and grated nutmeg

First, make the stuffing. Cook the swiss chard in boiling, salted water, until tender. Drain, then squeeze out as much water as possible and chop it finely.

Mash the ricotta in a basin and then add the swiss chard, parmesan, breadcrumbs, herbs, egg, salt, pepper and nutmeg and mix together.

Stuff the chicken with the ricotta mixture; sew up the opening with cook's string to enclose the stuffing. Put the chicken in a large flameproof casserole or saucepan with plenty of salted water, the sliced onion, celery and carrot, and cook for 30 minutes. Check that the chicken is cooked by piercing the thigh with a skewer; the juices should run clear.

Transfer the chicken to a warmed serving dish and carve at the table. The cooking liquid makes a wonderful soup or can be used as stock for another dish.

POLLO AI SEMI DI FINOCCHIO

CHICKEN WITH WILD FENNEL SEEDS

In Tuscany, chicken is nearly always cooked with some herbs; even when roasting chicken we use sage or rosemary. This recipe was made by my aunt Marina. She would make it on 8 September for the Feast of the Madonna. At this time of year, fennel seeds have only just been dried, so they still have a very strong flavour. If you don't have fennel seeds, you could use caraway seeds instead.

Serves 4

1.5kg/3lb chicken
1 garlic clove
200ml/7fl oz/scant 1 cup olive oil
½ tsp fennel seeds, crushed
salt and freshly ground black pepper

For the stuffing:
150g/5oz/1¼ cups chopped pancetta or streaky bacon
2 garlic cloves, chopped
1 tsp chopped fresh parsley
2 fresh sage leaves
1 tsp fennel seeds, crushed

Dry the chicken very thoroughly. Put the garlic clove into the olive oil and leave for an hour. Preheat the oven to 180°C/350°F/Gas Mark 4 or light the barbecue or a wood fire.

To make the stuffing, mix the pancetta or bacon with the chopped garlic, parsley, sage leaves and fennel seeds.

Season inside the chicken with salt and pepper, then stuff it with most of the pancetta mixture. Seal the opening with cook's string or a skewer. Add a little more stuffing at the neck end and put the chicken on a rotating spit, if possible, for cooking on the barbecue.

Season the outside of the chicken generously with salt, pepper and fennel seeds. Brush it with the garlic-flavoured oil, then grill, preferably over a wood fire, or cook in the oven. Brush with more oil from time to time. Cook it on the barbecue for about 40 minutes or until golden brown; on a rotating spit, the chicken may be cooked a little more quickly. If cooking in the oven, it will take 25–30 minutes. Check that the chicken is cooked by piercing the thickest part of the thigh with a skewer; the juices should run clear.

Carve at the table.

POLLO
ALL'ARETINA

ARETINA CHICKEN

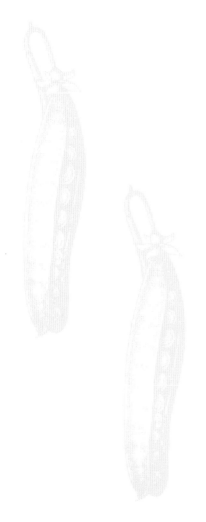

This dish takes its name from Aretum, a town south-east of Florence and the birthplace of Michelangelo.

My grandmother always made this with quite an old chicken. Nowadays, of course, you would use a young one. I remember this dish particularly because the juices of the chicken made a delicious sauce that was wonderful for dipping your bread into!

Serves 6

1.2kg/2lb 8oz chicken
250ml/9fl oz/generous 1 cup dry white wine
2 large onions, chopped
chicken or light meat stock
300g/11oz risotto rice, preferably Italian arborio
40g/1½ oz/¼ cup butter
300g/11oz/¾ cup shelled fresh peas
salt and freshly ground black pepper

Cut the chicken into pieces and then dry them.

Pour half the wine into a frying-pan (skillet) and cook the onions in it until softened. Add the chicken pieces and cook until lightly browned.

Season with salt and pepper and add the remaining wine. Continue cooking, adding a little hot stock now and again, for about 30 minutes.

Meanwhile, par-boil the rice for a few minutes. Drain it well.

Melt the butter in a frying-pan (skillet), stir in the rice, season with salt and pepper and add enough hot stock to cover the surface of the rice; then add the peas. From this point, you proceed as with risotto (see page 164), stirring frequently and adding more hot stock as the rice absorbs it.

When the rice is cooked, add the rice and peas to the chicken and stir well for 2–3 minutes. Check that the seasoning is to your taste and serve directly from the pan.

QUAGLIE IN FAGOTTO

BAKED QUAILS IN BREAD PARCELS

The reason why we cook quail in these bread parcels is to keep the gamey flavour of the quails. The bread is not supposed to be eaten, but it is no sin if you do! My cousin Juliano gave me this recipe. He runs a restaurant in the hills above Florence, and is a keen hunter and a wonderful cook.

Serves 4

8 quails
24 fresh sage leaves
4 fresh bay leaves
butter
about 16 bacon rashers
250g/9oz bread dough (see La Schiacciata, page 38)
2 tbsp olive oil
salt and freshly ground black pepper

Preheat the oven to 180°C/350°F/Gas Mark 4. Dry the quails very well. Stuff each quail with salt, pepper, a sage leaf, half a bay leaf and a knob of butter. Season the outsides with salt and pepper, then wrap each quail in bacon rashers, tucking in a couple more sage leaves.

Knead the bread dough and blend 2 tbsp of oil into it. Roll out fairly thinly and cut out eight pieces, each large enough to wrap a quail. Wrap each quail in dough, carefully sealing all the joins.

Butter an ovenproof dish and place the quail parcels in it. Brush each parcel with melted butter and bake for approximately 30 minutes. The cooking juices will flavour the dough 'wrapping', which will be delicious.

OCA AL FORNO

OVEN-BAKED GOOSE

Serves 6

1 goose, weighing about 3.6–4.5kg/8–10lb
olive oil
fresh rosemary sprigs
fresh sage leaves
black peppercorns, crushed
coarse salt
200ml/7fl oz/scant 1 cup dry white wine

For the stuffing:
1 onion, chopped
2 fresh sage leaves
salt, pepper and grated nutmeg
about 750g/1½lb crustless bread (the soft part
   of bread)
about 600ml/1 pint chicken or light meat stock
handful of green olives, stoned and chopped
2 garlic cloves, chopped
good pinch each of chopped fresh parsley,
   thyme and bay leaves

We used to cook this dish on the day of the wheat harvest, or on Christmas Day. At Christmas, we would make about 10 different courses and this would be the fourth course, after crostini and antipasti, soup with tortellini and a fish dish. After the goose, we would eat six or seven sweet things! If you started at 2 o'clock, you would not move from the table until well into the night.

Preheat the oven to 190°C/375°F/Gas Mark 5. Put aside the goose liver. Singe the bird if there are any remaining feather stumps, and then wash the goose, if necessary.

To make the stuffing, put some oil in a frying-pan (skillet) and fry the onion and 2 sage leaves, until the onion is soft.

Meanwhile, mince (grind) the goose liver. Stir it into the pan with the onion and sage, season with salt and a pinch of nutmeg and cook for 8 minutes.

Soak the bread in enough of the stock to moisten it, then squeeze out any liquid.

Transfer the mixture from the frying-pan (skillet) to a bowl, remove the sage leaves and mix in the softened bread, olives, garlic, a pinch each of the herbs, salt and plenty of pepper.

Stuff the goose with the mixture, sew up the bird with cook's string and lay it in an oiled, large, deep ovenproof dish. Sprinkle the goose with the leaves from the sprigs of rosemary and sage leaves, some crushed peppercorns and coarse salt. Cover it with a tent of foil to prevent the seasonings from falling off.

Roast, turning and basting at regular intervals, for about an hour if it is a 3.6kg/8lb bird. (For larger geese, add an extra 10 minutes for every 450g/1lb extra weight.) Pour off the fat once or twice during cooking, if necessary.

When the goose is well roasted, sprinkle with the wine to moisten it and make it easy to remove the skin. (If you like to eat crisp goose skin, however, omit this step.)

ANATRA ALL'ARETINA

ARETINA DUCK

This dish was cooked during harvest time. I remember that the person who made it best was a fellow who worked in the olive mill. We used to bring him the duck and he would cook it like this on an open fire. I don't know if it was the ambience or the meal itself, but this was the most fantastic thing I ever remember!

Serves 4

1.2kg/2lb 8oz duck
90ml/3fl oz/scant ½ cup olive oil
1 onion, chopped
1 carrot, chopped
1 celery stick, chopped
fresh sage leaves
150g/5oz prosciutto crudo (raw, cured ham), chopped
175ml/6fl oz/¾ cup dry white wine
600g/1lb ripe tomatoes, skinned, de-seeded and puréed
chicken or light meat stock
salt and freshly ground black pepper

Make sure that you remove the gland by the duck's tail, which would give a bitter taste. Cut the duck into pieces and dry with a clean teatowel.

Put the oil in a flameproof casserole and sauté the onion, carrot and celery with a few sage leaves. Add the prosciutto and, after a few minutes, the duck pieces. Brown them all over, season with salt and pepper and then pour in the wine. Raise the heat to evaporate the alcohol, then add the tomatoes.

Cook for around 1–1½ hours, frequently adding a little stock to prevent the dish from drying out.

FAGIANO AL CARTOCCIO

ROAST PHEASANT IN PAPER PARCELS

My cousin Juliano gave me this dish. He really is the greatest game cook I have ever met. As in the recipe for Quaglie in Fagotto (see page 94), we cook the pheasant in parcels – here made of paper rather than bread – to retain the gamey taste. In fact, game in Italy does not hang for as long as it does in England. We never eat game which has hung for more than three or four days.

Serves 4

1 pheasant
butter
3 juniper berries
fresh sage leaves
2 garlic cloves
50g/2oz prosciutto crudo (raw cured ham), minced (ground)
100g/4oz pancetta or bacon
fresh rosemary leaves
caul fat
salt and freshly ground black pepper

Preheat the oven to 180°C/350°F/Gas Mark 4. Wash the pheasant if necessary, and leave to drain for a few minutes. Stuff it with a knob of butter, the juniper berries, a few sage leaves, the garlic cloves, prosciutto and a pinch of salt.

Season the bird with salt and pepper, then wrap it in slices of pancetta or bacon, tucking in a few sage and rosemary leaves and tying the bacon in place with cook's string.

Blanch the caul fat briefly in boiling water to soften it, then leave it to drain for a few minutes. Wrap the pheasant in the fat and then in one layer of baking parchment paper and one of foil.

Put the pheasant in an ovenproof dish and roast for 40 minutes. Remove the wrappings, transfer to a warmed platter and serve.

FAGIANO ALLA PANCETTA

PHEASANT WITH PANCETTA

I include this recipe purely for the competition between two brothers – my cousins Juliano and Romano. I have already given you some of Juliano's recipes, so here is one of Romano's. Today, he is the head chef of the hotel school at Montecatini and is an excellent cook.

Serves 4

1–1.2kg/2–2½lb pheasant
200g/7oz pancetta or bacon, minced (ground), plus a few extra rashers
fresh sage leaves
salt and freshly ground black pepper

Preheat the oven to 180°C/350°F/Gas Mark 4. Wash the pheasant inside and out under running water if necessary, and leave for a while to dry.

Season the inside of the pheasant with salt and pepper and stuff it with the minced pancetta and a few sage leaves. Season the outside of the bird and wrap it with a few rashers of pancetta, tucking in a few more sage leaves; tie in place with cook's string.

Roast the pheasant in a buttered ovenproof dish for about 40 minutes, basting now and again with its own juice.

Remove the cook's string before serving; place the pheasant on a serving dish and pour the cooking juices over it.

FAGIANO AL TARTUFO NERO

PHEASANT WITH BLACK TRUFFLES

This recipe was given to me by a friend of mine called Armando, who, until he retired, was the chef at the hotel school in Montecatini and one of the greatest cooks of Tuscan cuisine.

Serves 4

1 pheasant
100g/4oz slices of prosciutto (ham), both fat and lean
30g/1oz black truffles
salt, pepper and grated nutmeg
150g/5oz pancetta or bacon
fresh sage leaves
butter for frying
3 garlic cloves
250ml/9fl oz/generous 1 cup dry white wine
150ml/5fl oz/⅝ cup double cream

Reserve the pheasant liver, if available. Wash the bird inside and out if necessary, and leave for a while to dry.

In a blender or food processor, mince (grind) the prosciutto with the truffles. Stuff the pheasant with this mixture.

Season the outside of the bird with salt and pepper, then wrap it in slices of pancetta or bacon, tucking in a few sage leaves and tying the bacon in place with cook's string.

Melt some butter in a large, shallow saucepan, add the garlic, a few more sage leaves and the pheasant. Brown thoroughly. Pour the wine over the pheasant and finish cooking, sprinkling with more wine should it dry out. It should take about 40 minutes.

Once cooked, lift the pheasant from the saucepan and remove the bacon. Cut the bird into pieces and place on a warmed serving dish. Spoon out the stuffing. Keep the joints warm while you make the sauce.

Mince (grind) the liver, if using. Remove the garlic and sage from the pheasant cooking juices and add the liver to the pan. Sprinkle with nutmeg and salt to taste, then add the stuffing. Stir with a wooden spoon for a few minutes.

Add the cream and stir gently for about 4 minutes. Then remove the sauce from the heat and pour it through a sieve. Pour some of the sauce over the pheasant and serve the remaining separately, in a sauce boat.

CONIGLIO ALLA CACCIATORA

HUNTER'S RABBIT

This recipe was one of my mother's specialities. I often cook it at home today and I still love it – the sauce, the gravy, the flavour – everything! Serve it with polenta or roasted potatoes.

Serves 6

1 rabbit, weighing about 2kg/4lb, jointed into 12 pieces
6 garlic cloves
3 large fresh rosemary sprigs
½ tsp salt
½ tsp freshly ground black pepper
75ml/3fl oz/scant ½ cup olive oil
½ bottle red wine
1 tbsp tomato purée (paste)
300ml/10fl oz/1¼ cups warm water

Wash the rabbit pieces if necessary, and dry them.

Chop ½ a garlic clove and the leaves from a sprig of rosemary and mix them with the salt and pepper. Rub this all over the rabbit joints. Cut another couple of garlic cloves into thin slivers. Make slits in the rabbit all over and and push some garlic slivers and more rosemary leaves into them.

Heat the oil in a large pan with the remaining garlic and the rest of the rosemary. Fry the rabbit joints all over until brown. Add the red wine gradually, so the temperature stays high enough to prevent the cooking from stopping.

Stir in the tomato purée (paste) and warm water.

Simmer gently until cooked, about 45 minutes.

CONIGLIO IN TEGAME

RABBIT IN TOMATO AND WINE SAUCE

This is one of my mother's recipes. She was a very good cook anyway, but when she made this dish she was the best ever! We used to eat it quite often for Sunday lunch. My father loved it, as he adored anything roasted or grilled. Rabbit is extremely popular in Tuscany, and this dish is a very common one.

Serves 4

1 rabbit, weighing about 1kg/2lb
wine vinegar
olive oil for frying
3 garlic cloves, chopped
1 fresh rosemary sprig
90ml/3fl oz/scant ½ cup dry white wine
90ml/3fl oz/scant ½ cup water
salt and freshly ground black pepper

Wash the rabbit, adding a little vinegar to the water. Cut it into joints and pat them dry with a clean teatowel.

Heat some oil in a casserole and sauté the garlic and rosemary until the garlic is lightly browned. Stir in the rabbit joints and cook until evenly browned; then season with salt and pepper and sprinkle with the wine. Simmer over a gentle heat and when the wine has evaporated, add the water.

Cook for about 30–40 minutes, adding small amounts of hot water if necessary to prevent the rabbit from drying out.

LEPRE ALL' AGRODOLCE

SWEET AND SOUR HARE

Serves 6

1 medium-sized hare, weighing about
   2.7–3.6kg/6–8lb
900ml/1½ pints/3½ cups dry white wine
175ml/6fl oz/¾ cup wine vinegar
1 onion, sliced
1 celery stick, sliced
1 carrot, sliced
1 garlic clove, sliced
2 cloves
3 juniper berries
black peppercorns
bouquet garni of parsley, sage, and rosemary
   sprigs and bay leaves
olive oil for frying
1 tbsp chopped fresh parsley
2 bay leaves
50g/2oz pancetta or bacon, finely chopped
350g/12 oz ripe tomatoes, de-seeded and
   roughly chopped
game or chicken stock

For the sweet and sour sauce:
1 tbsp water
2 tbsp sugar
50g/2oz bitter chocolate, grated
2 tbsp vinegar
50g/2oz raisins
75g/3oz pine nuts
30g/1oz candied orange and citron peel,
   chopped

Maria, my grandmother from my father's side, used to make this. I think she used to make it only for my father because he loved sweet and sour dishes. It took me a while to get accustomed to the taste, which is not all that common in Tuscany. If you can't find hare you can use anything with a gamey flavour such as fillet of venison. This is normally eaten on 8 September, the Feast of the Madonna, to celebrate the Immaculate Conception.

Wash the hare if necessary, cut it into joints and pat dry. Put the hare joints in a deep bowl and add 700ml/1¼ pints/2⅔ cups of the wine, vinegar, onion, celery, carrot, garlic, cloves, juniper berries, a few peppercorns and the bouquet garni. Leave to marinate for 24 hours.

Drain the hare joints and dry them. Remove the bouquet garni and chop the sprigs of herbs. Put a little oil in an earthenware or other heavy, flameproof casserole and sauté the chopped herbs from the marinade with the parsley, bay leaves and pancetta, until soft. Then add the hare joints and cook until browned all over. Pour in the remaining wine and raise the heat to evaporate it; then add the tomatoes and leave to simmer, adding a little hot stock occasionally to prevent the dish from drying out.

To make the sweet and sour sauce, put the water and sugar in a saucepan and cook until golden; then add the chocolate and, once this has melted, add the vinegar. Cook for 2 minutes and then add the raisins, pine nuts and candied peel. Stir thoroughly and remove from the heat.

When the meat is tender, remove the casserole from the heat. Sieve the meat cooking juices. Pour them back over the hare and gently stir in the sweet and sour sauce. Cook for a further 10 minutes, to allow all the flavours to blend, and then serve.

FEGATINI CON FUNGHI TRIFOLATI

CHICKEN LIVERS WITH PORCINI

Chicken liver is very common all over Tuscany because, as well as being cheap, once it has been eaten as a main course, you can chop up the leftovers and use them to make a pasta sauce for tagliatelle or purée them to make crostini.

Serves 4

400g/14oz chicken livers
400g/14oz fresh porcini mushrooms
50g/2oz/4 tbsp butter
2 garlic cloves, chopped
1 tbsp chopped fresh parsley
5 tbsp dry white wine
1 onion, chopped
fresh sage leaves
salt, pepper and nutmeg

Clean the chicken livers and slice them. Clean the mushrooms, wash and dry them. Slice them.

Melt half the butter in a frying-pan (skillet) and sauté the garlic and parsley; when golden, add the mushrooms. Cook for a few minutes and then add salt and pepper. Sprinkle with 2 tbsp of wine and finish cooking.

Put the rest of the butter in a saucepan and cook the onion and sage until wilted; then add the chicken livers. Season with salt, pepper and nutmeg and sprinkle with the remaining wine. Cook for 7–10 minutes, according to your taste; the livers should still be pink.

Serve the chicken livers on a warmed platter, garnished with the mushrooms.

MEAT

THE TUSCANS ARE WELL KNOWN AS MEAT EATERS. INDEED, ONE OF THE BEST TYPES OF BEEF IN THE WORLD COMES FROM TUSCANY – CHIANINA. IN TRADITIONAL TUSCAN CUISINE, BEEF WAS ONLY FOR THE RICH; STEAK WAS BEYOND MOST PEOPLE'S POCKETS. SO WE BOILED AND STEWED WHAT BEEF WAS AVAILABLE TO US AND THESE DISHES, SUCH AS SPEZZATINO ALLA FIORENTINA (SEE PAGE 106), HAVE BECOME DELICACIES OF TUSCAN CUISINE TODAY. OF COURSE, STEAK WAS, AND STILL IS, USED FOR SPECIAL OCCASIONS, IN SUCH DISHES AS BISTECCA ALLA FIORENTINA (SEE PAGE 112), WHICH IS SPECIALLY COOKED FOR A PICNIC ON THE FESTA DEL GRILLO, THE FEAST OF THE CRICKET, HELD ON ASCENSION DAY.

SPEZZATINO ALLA FIORENTINA

FLORENTINE BEEF STEW

This is one of the many Tuscan stews made from beef. Any leftover sauce is delicious on top of pasta.

Serves 4–6

90ml/3fl oz/scant ½ cup olive oil
800g/1lb 12oz lean stewing steak, cubed
4 garlic cloves
fresh rosemary leaves
175ml/6fl oz red wine
500g/1lb 2oz ripe tomatoes, skinned and chopped
salt and freshly ground black pepper

Heat the oil in a saucepan, add the meat, garlic and rosemary and brown the meat all over.

Pour the red wine over the meat and stir thoroughly, scraping the bottom of the pan to deglaze it. Raise the heat and continue cooking until most of the wine has evaporated.

Add the tomatoes and season with salt and pepper. Lower the heat, cover and simmer until the meat has become very tender; this should take just under 3 hours. Should the sauce reduce too much, add a little warm water. Make sure to stir regularly throughout the cooking time.

FETTINE DI MANZO SEMI COTTE

HALF-COOKED SLICES OF BEEF

When we could afford to buy good meat, my mother would make this dish. She would buy a piece of very lean meat and cut it into small pieces, then beat it until it was very thin – you could almost see through it! Then she would barely cook it, and we would eat it with lots of olive oil over the top. In this way she could feed six people with just one piece of good beef. We would dip lots of hot bread into the sauce and feel very full at the end!

Serves 4

1kg/2lb 4oz fillet of beef, cut into 12 slices
75ml/3fl oz/scant ½ cup olive oil
4 garlic cloves, crushed
175ml/6fl oz/¾ cup dry white wine
salt and freshly ground black pepper

Take the slices of beef and lay them between two sheets of strong, clear plastic, such as a freezer bag (cling film is too thin and will stick to the meat). Beat with a meat mallet to make the meat as thin as possible.

Heat four heatproof plates under the grill or in the oven until they are as hot as possible. Lay three slices of beef on each plate.

Heat the olive oil and garlic together until sizzling hot. Whisk in the wine and heat again almost to boiling point. Discard the garlic and pour the sauce evenly over the four portions of beef. Sprinkle with salt and pepper and serve at once.

STRACOTTO ALLA FIORENTINA

FLORENTINE BRAISED BEEF

This dish is equivalent to the British tradition of roast beef. It is very well cooked and marinated in wine so that the sauce is rich and dark – almost black. It is a dish we used to eat on feast days.

Serves 6

1kg/2lb 4oz braising steak or brisket
2 garlic cloves, thinly sliced
450g/1lb pancetta or bacon, cut into small pieces
90ml/3fl oz/scant ½ cup olive oil
1 onion, chopped
1 carrot, chopped
1 celery stick, chopped
175ml/6fl oz/¾ cup red wine
500g/1lb 2oz ripe tomatoes, skinned, de-seeded and puréed
light beef stock
salt and freshly ground black pepper

Pierce the meat all over with the point of a sharp, thin-bladed knife and insert the strips of garlic and the pieces of pancetta or bacon, sprinkled with pepper, into the holes. Tie the meat with cook's string so that it will keep its shape during cooking.

Put the oil in a casserole and fry the onion, carrot and celery until tender. Add the meat and cook until browned all over; then pour in the red wine.

After about 10 minutes, add the tomatoes. Season to taste with salt and pepper and simmer on a very low heat for about 4 hours, adding a little hot stock occasionally, to prevent the dish from drying out.

When the meat is cooked, remove the cook's string, place on a warmed platter, slice the meat, pour the gravy over it and serve.

STRACOTTO CON CIPOLLE

BEEFSTEAK CASSEROLE

This dish was originally made by my mother. My sister has made a more elegant recipe by using steak – my mother used to use lean meat. When we stew beef, we tend to cook it for quite some time: stracotto implies that this dish is overcooked, but the long cooking time makes the meat deliciously tender.

Serves 6

1kg/2lb 4oz beef topside or rump steak
2 garlic cloves, thinly sliced
50g/2oz pancetta or bacon, cut in thin strips
black peppercorns, crushed
175ml/6fl oz/¾ cup olive oil plus 2 tbsp
1 carrot, chopped
1 celery stick, chopped
1 tbsp chopped fresh parsley
1kg/2lb 4oz onions, sliced
1 tbsp tomato purée (paste), diluted in hot stock
90ml/3fl oz/scant ½ cup red wine
light meat stock
salt and freshly ground black pepper

Use a sharp, thin-bladed knife to make slits in the meat all over. Spike the meat with slices of garlic, using one clove. Roll pieces of pancetta or bacon in crushed peppercorns and then push the pancetta into the slits in the beef.

Heat 2 tbsp oil in a flameproof casserole and then brown the meat all over.

Meanwhile, heat the remaining olive oil in another saucepan and add the carrot, celery, remaining garlic clove, parsley and onions. Add the diluted tomato purée (paste) and cook until the onions are well softened.

Once the meat is browned all over, season it with salt and pepper and pour the wine over it. Continue cooking until the wine has evaporated; then add the sautéed vegetables.

Simmer for about 4 hours, adding hot stock from time to time to prevent the meat from drying out.

Serve the meat on the bed of vegetables on a warmed platter.

TAGLIATA DI MANZO

SLICED FILLET OF BEEF WITH

CORN SALAD

This first time I saw this dish, it had been prepared by Signora Guidotti, who lived next door to me. Corn salad in Italian is known as valeriana – I used to think it was medicinal, so when I saw people eating it I was very surprised. This recipe is served 'not-too-hot': this is because it is sprinkled with balsamic vinegar and olive oil after cooking. The vinegar and oil make a sauce that is poured on the hot meat.

Serves 4

1.2kg/2lb 8oz fillet of beef, carefully trimmed
6 handfuls of corn salad (lamb's lettuce) or watercress
8 tbsp olive oil
4 tbsp balsamic vinegar
salt and freshly ground black pepper

Cut the beef into four equal pieces. Fry them all on both sides for a minute or two in a cast-iron or other heavy-based frying-pan (skillet), without adding any fat. They must be very rare indeed.

Slice each fillet diagonally into 5mm/$1/4$-inch slices.

Arrange the corn salad on a platter and lay the slices of meat on top.

To the pan, which is still very hot indeed, add the oil, balsamic vinegar, salt and pepper. Stir this all together to make a thick, hot sauce and pour it all over the salad and meat. Serve at once.

BISTECCA ALLA FIORENTINA

FLORENTINE STEAK

There are many explanations for the origins of the word bistecca, *the Italian for beef steak. The most likely is that the prefix* bi, *meaning two, refers to the fact that a* bistecca *is made up of two cuts of meat, fillet and sirloin.* Stecca *is the forked wooden spit on which the meat roasts before the fire. The word* Bistecca *therefore means 'two on a stick' and the word can be found in cookery texts from the tenth and eleventh centuries. In the old days, the meat was cooked in front of the fire on a long wooden fork stuck in the ground; the steak cooked without being flooded by fat.*

The first time I ate this was on Ascension Day in the middle of May. I was out in the open air on the Montealbano hill with my family and my cousins and, this time, my father was the cook.

Serves 2

750g/1lb 10oz T-bone steak
175ml/6fl oz/¾ cup olive oil
leaves of 2 fresh rosemary sprigs
2 garlic cloves, crushed
salt and freshly ground black pepper

Marinate the steak for 24–48 hours in the olive oil, rosemary and garlic.

It should then be grilled over charcoal on a barbecue for about 4 minutes on each side. Season it with salt and pepper, according to taste. It should be served very rare.

POLPETTONE ALLA CONTADINA

PEASANT BEEF MEATLOAF

This dish is also known as 'fool's roast beef, because, if there was not enough money to buy a full joint, it would be cooked and sliced just like roast beef. When my grandmother used to make this we used to call it 'home-made' roast beef.

Serves 4

For the meatloaf:
soft part of 3 stale bread rolls
milk
500g/1lb 2oz minced (ground) beef
100g/4oz prosciutto crudo (raw cured ham), minced (ground)
70g/2½ oz/generous ½ cup grated parmesan cheese
2 eggs
salt, pepper and grated nutmeg
fresh white breadcrumbs for coating

For the sauce:
175ml/6fl oz/¾ cup olive oil
1 onion, chopped
1 celery stick, chopped
1 carrot, chopped
few tablespoons dry white wine
500g/1lb 2oz ripe tomatoes, skinned, de-seeded and puréed

To make the meatloaf
Soak the bread in a little milk and then squeeze out the excess liquid. In a bowl, mix the minced (ground) beef with the prosciutto, parmesan, softened bread and eggs; season with salt, pepper and nutmeg. When all the ingredients are well combined, shape the mixture into a large 'sausage' and coat it in breadcrumbs.

To make the sauce
Put the oil in a large saucepan and cook the onion, celery and carrot until wilted; then add the 'sausage'. Brown it on all sides, then sprinkle with the wine and, when this has evaporated, add the tomatoes.

Cover and simmer for about an hour, turning the 'sausage' around occasionally.

Serve on a platter, sliced and covered with the sauce.

SALSICCE CON LE RAPE O SPINACI

ITALIAN SAUSAGES WITH TURNIP TOPS
OR SPINACH

*Italian sausages should be made of 100 per cent meat, with no
cereal. The meat – either pork or turkey – should be coarse-cut
and seasoned with herbs and spices. The type of seasoning varies
from village to village, but the base should be salt and pepper.
At home, we used to make our own sausages and preserve them
in olive oil or lard so that they would keep all year round. Turnip
tops or spinach are the usual alternative to beans as the vegetable
accompaniment to sausages.*

Serves 4

500g/1lb 2oz turnip tops or spinach
3 tbsp olive oil
500g/1lb 2oz *salsicce* (Italian sausages)
90ml/3fl oz/scant ½ cup hot water
2 garlic cloves, chopped
salt and freshly ground black pepper

Wash the turnip tops or spinach, then cook in the water clinging
to the leaves, just until wilted. Drain and squeeze to get rid of the
excess water.

Heat the oil in a flameproof casserole over a low heat and cook
the sausages for 5 minutes. Pierce them with a fork to let the fat
ooze out and sprinkle with the hot water to prevent them from
sticking to the pan. When done, lift them from the casserole,
reserving the fat, and keep warm.

Add a little more oil to the fat of the sausages if necessary,
add the garlic, and fry the turnip tops or spinach until done.

Add salt and pepper to taste, stir well, add the sausages, cook
for a further 10 minutes and serve.

SPIEDINO UCCELLI SCAPPATI

KEBABS OF WILD BOAR SAUSAGES

WITH CHICKEN

In this recipe, the sausages are skewered like kebabs. In Tuscany, we used to cook thrushes in the same way, so this dish is called Uccelli Scappati or 'fly away birds'. It tastes as gamey as the thrushes would have done if they had been cooked instead.

Serves 6

3 boneless, skinless chicken breasts
12 fresh wild boar sausages
24 large fresh sage leaves
12 cubes of bread, about 4cm/1½ inches square
olive oil
extra-virgin olive oil, to serve

Preheat the oven to 190°C/375°F/Gas Mark 5.

Cut the chicken breasts into six pieces and roll each one up into a sausage shape.

Make up each skewer following this sequence: first sausage, then sage, a bread cube, sage, chicken, sage, bread, sage, sausage.

Coat the six skewers with olive oil, place them in an ovenproof dish, resting the skewers on the edge of the dish so that the food does not touch the bottom of the dish, and roast them for about 25 minutes.

Before serving sprinkle them with some extra-virgin olive oil.

TRIPPA ALLA FIORENTINA

FLORENTINE TRIPE

I used to save up to go to the cinema by doing odd jobs here and there. When we came out of the cinema in the winter, there was a man selling this dish from a little trolley, and we used to buy some and warm our hands around it. The Tuscans have a tradition of eating tripe – although in the past it was a poor man's food, it has now become chic and you can find it in many restaurants in Florence.

Serves 4

800g/1lb 12oz tripe, already cooked
90ml/3fl oz/scant ½ cup olive oil
1 onion, chopped
1 carrot, chopped
1 celery stick, chopped
500g/1lb 2oz ripe tomatoes, skinned de-seeded and puréed, or canned tomatoes
50g/2oz/½ cup grated parmesan cheese
salt and freshly ground black pepper

Wash the tripe in plenty of water and then blanch it for around 10 minutes in boiling water. Drain it and cut it into strips.

Put the oil in a casserole and fry the onion, carrot and celery until tender. Add the tripe, cook for a few more minutes and then add the tomatoes. Cover and simmer for about 30 minutes, seasoning with some salt and pepper halfway through.

If you find that, towards the end of cooking time, the cooking juices have not thickened sufficiently, take the lid off and raise the heat for a few minutes.

Add the grated parmesan just before removing from the heat; serve piping hot.

FEGATO ALLA FIORENTINA

FLORENTINE CALVES' LIVER

The propietor of a restaurant in Florence called La Bettola gave me this recipe. His restaurant is very popular with students, who like to order this dish as it is not too expensive.

Serves 4

600g/1lb 5oz calves' liver, very thinly sliced
plain (all-purpose) white flour, for coating
90ml/3fl oz/scant ½ cup olive oil
2 garlic cloves
about 6 fresh sage leaves
salt

Ask your butcher to slice the liver thinly for you. Coat the slices in flour.

Heat the oil in a frying-pan (skillet) and sauté the garlic and sage for a few minutes until they have flavoured the oil. Remove the garlic and sage and then add the slices of liver and fry them quickly, for 1–2 minutes on each side.

Season with salt before removing from the heat; serve piping hot.

FRITTO MISTO DI CARNI

MIXED MEAT AND VEGETABLE FRITTERS

This is a dish which we would eat quite often at home. We would vary the meat that we used from time to time – you can use any meat you have to hand.

Serves 4

250g/9oz globe artichokes
lemon juice
4 lamb chops
250g/9oz chicken or rabbit liver or calves' liver, brains and sweetbread
4 small courgettes (zucchini), thinly sliced lengthways
olive oil for deep-frying
lemon slices, to garnish

For the batter:
2 eggs
salt and freshly ground black pepper
3 tbsp plain (all-purpose) white flour
1 tbsp olive oil
90ml/3fl oz/scant ½ cup dry white wine
grated nutmeg

Wash the artichokes, remove the tips and the hard outer leaves and soak them in water with a few drops of lemon juice for around 30 minutes.

Beat the lamb chops with a meat hammer.

If using brains and sweetbreads, wash them in plenty of cold water; then blanch them in salted, boiling water for a few minutes. Drain, remove the film around them and slice them thinly. Slice the liver thinly.

To make the batter, beat the eggs in a bowl, season with salt and pepper and stir in the flour, oil, wine and a pinch of nutmeg. Blend all the ingredients together until you have a fairly soft, smooth batter.

Dip the various meats in the batter and deep-fry in plenty of very hot oil for 7 minutes. Lift from the oil when ready and drain on kitchen paper.

Dip the courgettes (zucchini) and artichokes in the batter and deep-fry in the same way, but cook them for only 3 minutes.

Serve on a warmed platter, with slices of lemon.

ROGNONCINI ALL'ACETO BALSAMICO

CALVES' KIDNEYS WITH BALSAMIC
VINEGAR

This recipe was given to me by a colleague of mine who has a restaurant next to the market in Pistoia. This restaurant is renowned for having an exceptionally high number of offal dishes on the menu – people go there especially to eat offal.

Serves 4

500g/1lb 2oz calves' kidneys
2 eggs
plain (all-purpose) white flour for coating
olive oil for frying
salt and freshly ground black pepper
balsamic vinegar, to serve
lemon wedges, to garnish

Blanch the kidneys for a few minutes in boiling water.

Skin the kidneys by making a small incision and removing the two outer layers that cover the kidneys; then slice them thinly.

Beat the eggs with salt and pepper. Dip the kidneys in the egg and then coat them in flour. Fry in very hot oil for 5–6 minutes. You can cook them for a little longer, if you prefer, but do not overcook them.

Drain the kidneys on kitchen paper, sprinkle them with a few drops of vinegar and serve on a platter garnished with a wedge of lemon.

INVOLTINI DI VITELLO

VEAL AND SAUSAGE ENVELOPES

This is such a delicate dish that it was only eaten when someone in the family was unwell. We would eat it on the same day that we would eat the chicken broth (see page 18). I would like to tell all English readers that in Italy, if you say 'veal' you are asking for young beef, manzo, *or young ox. If you want to specify that you want veal as we understand it, you have to use the words* vitello *or* vitello di latte – *milk-fed veal.*

Serves 4

600g/1lb 5oz veal escalopes
150g/5oz *salsicce* (Italian sausages), sliced
fresh sage leaves
90ml/3fl oz/scant ½ cup dry olive oil
1 onion, chopped
1 garlic clove, chopped
1 carrot, chopped
1 celery stick, chopped
90ml/3fl oz/scant ½ cup dry white wine
500g/1lb 2oz ripe tomatoes, skinned, de-seeded and puréed
fresh basil leaves
hot water or stock (optional)
salt and freshly ground black pepper

Beat the escalopes with a meat mallet until they are thin. Place on each of them a piece of sausage and a sage leaf. Roll each slice of veal into a parcel and seal them with a wooden stick or with cook's string.

Heat the oil in a frying-pan (skillet) and sauté the onion, garlic, carrot and celery. Add the meat parcels and, when they are well blended with the vegetables, sprinkle with the wine. When the wine has evaporated, add the tomatoes and a few basil leaves. Season to taste with salt and pepper.

Simmer for a further 5 minutes, adding a little hot water or stock, if necessary, to prevent the dish from drying out.

UCCELLETTI FALSI

FOOL'S BIRDS

This is called 'fool's birds' because it is the same shape as little birds. Furthermore, anything made with sage acquires a gamey taste. So, this dish looks and tastes as if it is made with small game birds. This was a very popular dish with my mother. If I was asleep and I woke up to see this on the table, I would always think it was a Sunday!

Serves 4

600g/1lb 5oz topside of veal, sliced
prosciutto crudo (raw cured ham), sliced
fresh sage leaves
3 tbsp olive oil
2 garlic cloves
1 celery stick, chopped
1 carrot, chopped
90ml/3fl oz/scant ½ cup dry white wine
500g/1lb 2oz ripe tomatoes, skinned, de-seeded
   and roughly chopped
salt and freshly ground black pepper

Trim and flatten the meat slices with a mallet and place on each one a slice of prosciutto and a sage leaf. Roll up the slices and either close them using wooden cocktail sticks or tie them up with cook's string.

Heat the oil in a flameproof casserole and brown the garlic cloves, to flavour the oil. Remove the garlic and add the chopped celery, carrot and two sage leaves to the oil. Add the meat parcels and, when they are well sealed, sprinkle with salt and pepper and pour in the wine. Simmer over a low heat for 15 minutes.

Add the tomatoes and cook for a further 10 minutes, adding a very small amount of hot water if necessary to prevent them from drying out.

NODINO DI VITELLO AL POMODORO

VEAL CHOPS WITH TOMATO SAUCE

This is a dish that you will find quite often in Italian restaurants. Here, this cut of meat is cooked with a sauce. You can also cook veal steaks using just sage and butter.

Serves 4

4 veal steaks
olive oil for frying
salt and freshly ground black pepper

For the sauce:
3 tbsp olive oil
1 onion, chopped
1 garlic clove, chopped
350g/12oz ripe tomatoes, skinned, de-seeded and puréed
90ml/3fl oz/scant ½ cup red wine

To make the sauce, put the oil in a casserole and fry the onion and garlic until softened. Add the tomatoes, sprinkle with salt and pepper and cook for about 10 minutes more.

Pour in the wine and then leave to simmer for a further 10 minutes.

Meanwhile, cook the steaks in very little oil on both sides; season with salt and pepper and place on a warmed platter. Keep warm.

Pour the sauce over the steaks and serve at once.

ARROSTO DI VITELLO

ROAST VEAL

Every region in Italy has its own way of preparing this extremely well-known dish, which is as popular in Italy as roast beef is in England. This is the Tuscan way, which is quite simple and plain and uses the flavour of nutmeg, as well as milk to tenderize the meat. Roasted new potatoes are a very good accompaniment for this dish. I love it!

Serves 4

700–800g/1lb 9oz–1lb 12oz veal noisette (topside)
2 garlic cloves, chopped
large knob of butter
90ml/3fl oz/scant ½ cup wine vinegar
grated nutmeg
500ml/18fl oz/2½ cups cold milk
salt and freshly ground black pepper

Preheat the oven to 180°C/350°F/Gas Mark 4. Tie the meat with cook's string so that it will remain in one piece during cooking.

Sauté the garlic in a flameproof casserole with the butter for a few minutes; then add the meat. When this is browned all over, sprinkle with the vinegar and continue heating for a few minutes, to evaporate the vinegar fumes. Sprinkle with nutmeg and pour in the milk.

Cover, transfer to the oven and cook until ready, about 45 minutes, stirring and basting the meat occasionally. Season with salt and pepper not long before the end of cooking.

When done, pour the sauce into a warmed platter and lay the sliced veal on top.

ARISTA ALLA FIORENTINA

FLORENTINE ROAST LOIN OF PORK

This recipe dates back to an Ecumenical Council held in the 1250s. At that time, the bishops spoke Greek rather than Latin as a lingua franca. A meal was prepared for them from a loin of pork and, after the meal, everyone cried 'Aristo!' which, in Greek, means 'very good, excellent'; from that date this dish has been known as arista. *You can buy it in delicatessens in Florence to slice and eat in a sandwich.*

The chine is part of the loin of pork. Ask your butcher to detach the meat from the bone or to cut the bone in several places, in order to facilitate slicing.

Serves 8

1 chine of pork, weighing about 1.5–1.6kg/3–3½ lb
2 garlic cloves, finely chopped
1 tbsp chopped fresh rosemary leaves
salt and freshly ground black pepper

Preheat the oven to 180°C/350°F/Gas Mark 4.

If your meat has been detached from the bone, tie the meat to the bone before cooking for extra flavour.

Mix the garlic with the rosemary leaves and salt and pepper. Pierce the meat with a sharp, thin-bladed knife and insert the garlic mixture in the holes. Place the meat in an ovenproof dish and season it with plenty of salt and pepper.

Cook for 35 minutes. Make sure that during cooking you baste it regularly with its own juice.

Test the meat with a fork; it is done when the fork goes in easily. Slice and serve hot.

ARROSTO DI CINGHIALE

ROAST WILD BOAR

This dish was usually eaten in November and was often made by a lady named Arduina, one of my neighbours. You could use a loin of pork instead of wild boar, but you would have to marinate it in red wine for at least 48 hours beforehand.

Serves 6

1.2kg/2lb 8oz boneless, rolled loin of wild boar
6 garlic cloves, thinly sliced
100g/4oz pancetta or bacon
olive oil
175ml/6fl oz/¾ cup red wine
meat stock
salt and freshly ground black pepper

Preheat the oven to 180°C/350°F/Gas Mark 4.

Pierce the meat with a sharp, thin-bladed knife and insert the garlic in the holes.

Cover the joint with slices of pancetta sprinkled with pepper.

Heat the oil in a flameproof casserole. Brown the meat on all sides. When the meat is golden brown, pour the red wine over it. When this has evaporated, transfer to the oven and roast, turning often and adding a little hot stock at regular intervals to prevent it from drying out. Cook for about 35 minutes.

Test the meat with a fork; when it goes in easily, the meat is done.

AGNELLO AL FORNO

OVEN-BAKED LAMB

In Tuscany lamb is cooked as it is in Rome, when very young, only three or four days old. We refer to 'lamb' to mean a lamb which has been fed only on its mother's milk. The moment it starts to graze on grass, we call it 'mutton' – it may be young, but it is still mutton! I like to make this dish when I am at home on a Sunday.

Serves 6

1.2kg/2lb 8oz lamb (leg or shoulder)
3 garlic cloves, thinly sliced
3 or 4 fresh rosemary sprigs
250ml/9fl oz olive oil
1 tbsp wine vinegar
salt and freshly ground black pepper

Pierce the meat with the point of a sharp, thin-bladed knife and insert the strips of garlic and the rosemary sprigs into the holes; then season it with plenty of salt and pepper.

Put the lamb in a bowl with the olive oil and vinegar and leave to marinate for an hour, turning it frequently. Preheat the oven to 200°C/400°F/Gas Mark 6.

Place the meat in a roasting tin, cover it with the marinade and roast for about 15–20 minutes, keeping it moist by basting it with the cooking juices.

AGNELLO IN SALSA

LAMB CASSEROLE WITH PARSLEY

My grandmother used to be very good at making all kinds of stews, and she used to make this one quite often. In Tuscany, chilli pepper is used as a seasoning as often as black pepper.

Serves 6

90ml/3fl oz/scant ½ cup olive oil
2 garlic cloves, chopped
1 tsp chopped fresh parsley
1 dried red chilli, chopped
1 fresh rosemary sprig
1kg/2lb 4oz boneless casserole lamb, cut into chunks
90ml/3fl oz/scant ½ cup dry white wine
500g/1lb 2oz ripe tomatoes, skinned and chopped
salt and freshly ground black pepper

Heat the oil in a casserole and sauté the garlic, parsley, red chilli and rosemary.

Add the lamb and brown all over. Season with salt and pepper and sprinkle with wine. Raise the heat to evaporate the wine.

Add the tomatoes and simmer for 8–10 minutes, adding a little hot water from time to time as the juice dries out.

When ready, check the seasoning and serve.

AGNELLO MONTEALBANO

ROAST LEG OF LAMB WITH BLACK OLIVES

This dish is made on one of Tuscany's most beautiful hillsides, Montealbano, which divides the flats of Florence and Lucca. It is also the place where I was born, and is close to the famous town of Vinci, the birthplace of Leonardo da Vinci. The ingredients used are readily available in this part of Tuscany. I remember that a lady in my village called Nella used to make it – she was the mother of my best friend, Federico. When she cooked this, there was such a lovely smell that although she lived 400 metres away, I could still smell it!

Serves 6

3 tbsp olive oil
2.75kg/6lb leg of lamb
1 large onion, sliced
2 tbsp brandy
10 garlic cloves
1 beefsteak tomato, skinned, de-seeded and cut into strips
15 fresh thyme sprigs, tied in a bundle with string
150ml/5fl oz/⅝ cup red wine
175g/6oz black olives, rinsed and pitted
salt and freshly ground black pepper

Preheat the oven to 170°C/325°F/Gas Mark 3.

Heat the olive oil in a large, flameproof casserole and brown the lamb on all sides; remove from the dish.

Add the onion and cook until it begins to caramelize. Return the lamb to the pan. Heat the brandy in a ladle and ignite it with a match, then pour it over the lamb. You can do this 1 tbsp at a time if you are nervous of flambéeing.

Add the garlic, tomato, thyme and half the red wine; season with salt and pepper, then cover and cook in the oven for 1 hour, turning the leg halfway through.

Add the remaining wine and the olives to the casserole and return to the oven for another hour.

Take out of the oven and let the meat rest for 15 minutes.

Place the lamb on a plate and carve the meat. Skim the surface of the juices to remove excess fat and remove the thyme. Serve the juices with the lamb.

POLPETTE ALLA FIORENTINA

FLORENTINE MEATBALLS

This dish was traditionally made with leftovers. Mamma would mince the beef or veal in a great big terracotta bowl and create a new dish from an old one.

Serves 4–5

150g/5oz potatoes
200g/7oz stale country-style bread
milk
200g/7oz leftover boiled or roasted meat, minced (ground)
40g/1½ oz/scant ½ cup grated parmesan cheese
1 tbsp chopped fresh parsley
1 egg, beaten
salt, pepper and grated nutmeg
fresh white breadcrumbs for coating
olive oil for frying
lemon slices to garnish

Boil the potatoes whole, in their skins. Drain and leave to cool.

Peel the potatoes and push them through a mouli, potato ricer or sieve into a large bowl.

Meanwhile, soak the bread in the milk. When softened, squeeze out the excess milk.

Mix the minced (ground) meat, parmesan, parsley, egg, salt, pepper, nutmeg and the bread with the potatoes. Blend thoroughly and form into balls or any other shape you choose.

Coat the meatballs in the breadcrumbs and fry them in very hot oil for about 15 minutes.

When golden on all sides, drain them on kitchen paper and serve garnished with lemon slices.

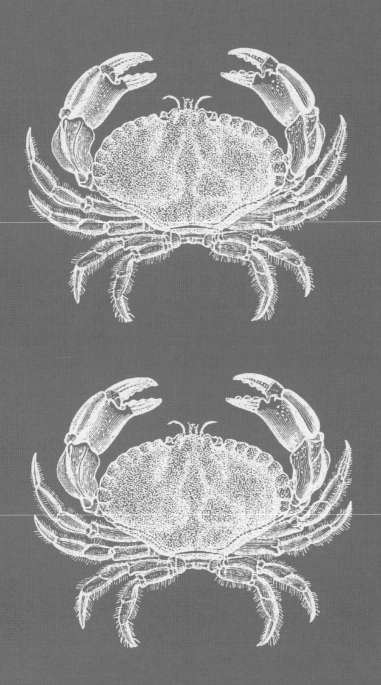

FISH AND SHELLFISH

I AM NOT A KEEN SEA-GOER, ALTHOUGH IN MY LIFE I HAVE CROSSED MANY OCEANS! HOWEVER, I LOVE TO EAT FISH, AND IT'S PROBABLY THE MAIN COURSE THAT I EAT MOST OFTEN NOW. AS A BOY I USED TO SWIM IN POOLS AND STREAMS ON THE HILLSIDES AND SOMETIMES WE WOULD DRY THE SMALLER POOLS OUT IN ORDER TO CATCH EEL. I WOULD TAKE THESE HOME FOR MY MOTHER TO COOK. THERE WAS A MAN WHO USED TO COME ROUND THE VILLAGE ON A THURSDAY AFTERNOON ON HIS BICYCLE WITH A BASKET OF FRESH FISH STRAIGHT FROM THE BOAT. HE WOULD COVER THE FISH IN FIG LEAVES – THIS WAS THE ONLY REFRIGERATION HE HAD. MAMMA WOULD COOK THE FISH ON FRIDAY. TUSCANY HAS A WIDE MENU OF FISH DISHES: THE TUSCAN COASTLINE IS THE LONGEST IN ITALY, AND TUSCANY ALSO INCLUDES ISLANDS SUCH AS ELBA. IN THIS BOOK, YOU WILL FIND A FEW RECIPES FOR SALT COD, WHICH IS A VERY COMMON FISH IN TUSCANY; IT IS EVEN COOKED BY THE SEA, BUT ONLY IN THE WINTER, WHEN FRESH FISH IS HARDER TO GET. TUSCANY HAS MANY RIVERS AND SO WE HAVE A LOT OF EEL AND TROUT RECIPES, BUT THESE RECIPES CAN BE USED FOR ANY FRESHWATER FISH.

ZUPPA DI COZZE

MUSSEL SOUP

I used to eat this soup as a boy when mussels were in season. It is one of the most common Tuscan dishes to be found in restaurants in Italy.

Serves 4

1.2kg/2lb 8oz live mussels
handful of chopped fresh parsley
chopped fresh parsley and lemon slices to garnish

For the tomato sauce:
90ml/3fl oz/scant ½ cup olive oil
2 garlic cloves, finely chopped
1 tbsp chopped fresh parsley
500g/1lb 2oz fresh ripe tomatoes, skinned, de-seeded and puréed
90ml/3fl oz/scant ½ cup dry white wine
4 slices of stale country-style bread
salt and freshly ground black pepper

First, make the sauce: put the oil in a flameproof casserole and sauté the garlic with the parsley. Add the tomatoes, season with salt and pepper and simmer for 15 minutes. Add a little hot water from time to time, to prevent the sauce from drying out.

Scrub and de-beard the mussels and wash them carefully in several changes of cold water. Discard any that do not close when sharply tapped.

Place the mussels in a saucepan over a medium heat, with the parsley. Cook until they have opened, shaking the pan occasionally. Discard any mussels that do not open and lift the rest into a bowl.

Strain the juices through a fine sieve into a second bowl.

Stir the mussels into the tomato sauce, until well mixed. Alternatively, for a soup that is more elegant to eat, remove the mussels from their shells before stirring them into the tomato sauce. Add the wine and the mussels' cooking juices. Simmer for about 10 minutes.

In the meantime, toast the slices of bread and place them at the bottom of four serving bowls. Pour the mussel soup into the bowls, sprinkle with parsley and serve with lemon slices.

VONGOLE AL POMODORO

CLAM SOUP

In my childhood, clams were readily available on the many beautiful beaches of the Tuscan coast. We would pick clams straight off the beach – this was before the sea became so polluted. Today, sadly, I would suggest you don't pick clams or any shellfish from the wild. In Tuscany, these clams are often seen on menus as arselle *rather than* vongole.

Serves 4

1.5kg/3lb clams in their shells

For the tomato sauce:
90ml/3fl oz/scant ½ cup olive oil
2 garlic cloves
750g/1½ lb ripe tomatoes, skinned and roughly chopped
1 tbsp chopped fresh parsley
salt and freshly ground black pepper

First, make the sauce: put the oil in a frying-pan (skillet) and sauté the garlic cloves until golden to flavour the oil; then remove them. Add the tomatoes and season with salt and pepper. Simmer over a very low heat for about 20 minutes. Add the parsley for the last 5 minutes.

Sieve the sauce.

Meanwhile, wash the clams in plenty of cold water and spread them out in a large saucepan. Cook over a medium to high heat, covered, shaking the pan occasionally, until they have all opened (discard any that don't open).

Remove from the heat, remove clams from the shells and place in a lightly oiled, flameproof casserole dish. Cover with the tomato sauce and cook for around 5 minutes. Serve immediately.

Tip:
You should never purée tomato sauce in a food processor or a liquidizer because the white stalk scar and core of the tomatoes, as well as the seeds, make processed or liquidized tomato sauce look yellow. Always purée tomatoes either using a mouli-légumes or through a wide-holed sieve, pushing the flesh through with the back of a spoon or a spatula.

POLIPI IN PADELLA

OCTOPUS WITH GARLIC SAUCE

I had a friend called Tito whose family used to come and stay with us in early spring. In the summer, we would return the visit and go to stay in their house in Viareggio. Tito's mother used to make this dish using the octopus she had bought fresh from the market that morning. In Tuscany, when you extend an invitation, you don't just say, 'When are you coming to stay?' – instead you say, 'When are you coming to eat the polipi?', or the calamari, or whatever it might be. This is what Tito's mother used to say to us!

Serves 4

500g/1lb 2oz small octopus
90ml/3fl oz/scant ½ cup olive oil
2 garlic cloves, finely chopped
1 tbsp chopped fresh parsley
salt and freshly ground black pepper
lemon slices to garnish

Peel off as much as possible of the octopus outer skin and cut out the eyes and the mouth opening and the yellow sac. Wash the bodies in plenty of running water and cut them into thin ribbons.

Put the oil in a frying-pan (skillet) and sauté the garlic and parsley for a few minutes.

Add the octopus and stir for 2–3 minutes. Season with salt and pepper, cover and simmer for about 15 minutes.

Serve hot, garnished with lemon slices.

OSTRICHE ALLA LIVORNESE

LIVORNESE OYSTERS

This recipe was given to me by the chef of a restaurant in Viareggio called L'Amico.

Serves 4

24 oysters
2 garlic cloves
2 tbsp chopped fresh parsley
1 small onion, finely chopped
salted anchovies, rinsed
handful of fresh white breadcrumbs
olive oil
salt
lemon slices to garnish

Preheat the oven to 140°C/275°F/Gas Mark 2. Wash the oysters, open them and discard the top shells.

In a pestle and mortar, crush the garlic, parsley, onion, anchovies and breadcrumbs, adding the ingredients gradually.

Trickle in the olive oil gradually, until you have a soft paste. Place a little on each oyster.

Arrange the oysters on a grill rack, transfer to the oven and cook for about 20 minutes.

Serve hot, garnished with lemon slices.

MUSCOLI RIPIENI ALLA PISTOIESE

STUFFED MUSSELS

Serves 4

1.2kg/2lb 8oz live mussels, as large
   as you can get
2 garlic cloves, chopped
1 tbsp chopped fresh parsley
fine white breadcrumbs for topping

For the stuffing:
150g/5oz *salsicce* (Italian sausages)
50g/2oz *mortadella* (soft, cured Italian pork
   sausage)
soft part of 1 bread roll
1 garlic clove, chopped
1 tsp chopped fresh parsley
1 egg, beaten
salt and freshly ground black pepper

For the sauce:
3 tbsp olive oil
1 onion, chopped
1 tsp chopped fresh parsley
500g/1lb 2oz fresh ripe tomatoes, skinned,
   de-seeded and puréed
salt and freshly ground black pepper

I call these mussels muscoli *because, in Tuscany, we have learnt this from the English! In the rest of Italy, mussels are always known as* cozze.

Preheat the oven to 180°C/350°F/Gas Mark 4.

To make the sauce: put the oil in a casserole and sauté the onion with the parsley for a few minutes. Add the tomatoes, salt and pinch of pepper and simmer for about 20 minutes. Then transfer to an oiled ovenproof dish.

To make the stuffing, mince (grind) the *salsiccia* and the *mortadella* together in a food processor. Soak the bread in water and then squeeze it dry. Mix the the sausages and bread together with the garlic, parsley and egg. Season with salt and a pinch of pepper.

Scrub and de-beard the mussels and wash them carefully in several changes of cold water. Discard any that do not close when sharply tapped.

Put the mussels into a saucepan over a medium heat with the garlic and parsley. Shake the pan from time to time and remove the mussels as they open up. Discard any that do not open.

Discard the top shells from the mussels and fill the lower shells with the stuffing. Arrange them on the tomato sauce and sprinkle with breadcrumbs.

Bake for 20 minutes; serve hot.

CALAMARI CON BIETOLE

SQUID WITH SWISS CHARD

My auntie Rimide used to cook this dish. I never had it at home because my father decreed that we could not eat any fish that did not look like a fish! In Tuscany, we only use swiss chard when it is very young and tender. Spinach is a good substitute.

Serves 4

600g/1lb 5 oz fresh squid
500g/1lb 2oz swiss chard
90ml/3fl oz/scant ½ cup olive oil
2 garlic cloves, chopped
1 onion, chopped
1 carrot, chopped
1 celery stick, chopped
1 tbsp chopped fresh parsley
1 small piece of dried red chilli
90ml/3fl oz/scant ½ cup dry white wine
350g/12oz fresh ripe tomatoes, skinned, de-seeded and puréed
salt and freshly ground black pepper

Clean the squid, slide the flat bone out of the body, remove the eyes and mouth, wash in plenty of running water and cut into thin ribbons.

Wash the chard, then cook in the water clinging to the leaves. Drain and chop roughly.

Put the oil in a flameproof casserole and sauté the garlic, onion, carrot, celery, parsley and chilli for a few minutes. Add the squid and stir to ensure that the flavours all blend together. Add the wine and, when this has evaporated, the chard.

Season with salt and pepper and, after a few minutes, add the tomatoes. Simmer for 30 minutes. Serve straight from the casserole.

SEPPIE CON PISELLI

CUTTLEFISH WITH PEAS

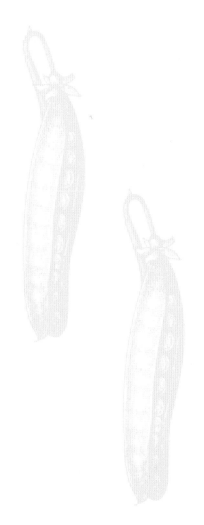

This dish was made by my aunt Adrianna when fresh peas were just in season. I used to pick them for her from the garden – they were so sweet and tender that I always ate some of them straight from the pod while I was picking.

Serves 4

600g/1lb 5oz cuttlefish
90ml/3fl oz/scant ½ cup olive oil
2 garlic cloves, chopped
1 tbsp chopped fresh parsley
1 small piece of dried red chilli
90ml/3fl oz/scant ½ cup dry white wine
500g/1lb 2oz fresh ripe tomatoes, skinned, de-seeded and puréed
700g/1lb 9oz fresh peas, shelled
salt and freshly ground black pepper

Clean the cuttlefish, remove the flat bone from the body, wash in plenty of running water and cut the body into thin ribbons.

Put the oil in an earthenware or heavy-based saucepan and sauté the garlic, parsley and chilli for a few minutes to flavour the oil.

Add the cuttlefish and, when the flavours are well blended, season with salt and pepper and sprinkle with the wine. When this has evaporated, add the tomatoes and simmer for about 2 hours, adding small amounts of hot water to prevent the dish from drying out.

After 2 hours, add the peas and cook for a further 30 minutes. Serve piping hot.

ZUPPA DI PESCE ALLA VERSIGLIESE

FISH SOUP

Versiglia is the seaside of Tuscany. This dish came from my Auntie Derna who came from that part of the world. This is the lazy way of making the local fish soup or Cacciucco (see page 163) – but I'm not being unkind to my aunt because making Cacciucco is really hard work. She always used to say that this was better than Cacciucco anyway!

Serve this in individual soup dishes, with triangles of toasted bread. Decorate with chopped parsley.

Serves 4

For the sauce:
90ml/3fl oz/scant ½ cup olive oil
1 garlic clove, chopped
½ onion, chopped
1 gurnard, cleaned and gutted
1 red mullet, cleaned and gutted
225g/8oz monkfish
2 large raw shell-on prawns
1 small crab
300ml/10fl oz/1¼ cups dry white wine
20g/¾ oz saffron strands
salt and freshly ground pepper

For the fish:
4 gurnard, cleaned, gutted and sliced
4 red mullet, weighing about 225g/8oz each, cleaned, gutted and sliced
8 slices of monkfish, weighing about 100g/4oz each
8 large prawns
8 small crabs
12 large mussels

First, make the sauce: heat the oil in a large pan and sauté the garlic and onion until golden. Add the fish, prawns and crab and cook for 10 minutes. Add the wine and saffron, cover and cook for 40 minutes more.

Season with salt and pepper. Remove from the heat and allow to cool. Remove and bone the fish.

Pass the sauce through a strainer. Liquidize or process the fish and sauce together.

Put the puréed fish sauce in a large pan and add the gurnard, red mullet, monkfish, prawns, crabs and mussels. Cook for 25 minutes to achieve the best fish soup in Tuscany!

BACCALA BIANCO

BOILED SALT COD

Baccala (salt cod) is part of Tuscany's staple diet. Although I have only given you three recipes in this book, there are plenty more. We love it because of its salty taste. My mother used to serve it with boiled potatoes drowned, rather than tossed, in olive oil!

Serves 4

500g/1lb 2oz salt cod
2 garlic cloves
1 fresh parsley sprig
90ml/3fl oz/scant ½ cup olive oil
freshly ground black pepper
country-style bread, to serve

Soak the salt cod overnight; the ideal way to do this is in gently running water but, if you don't want to do this, simply soak it in several changes of water.

Rinse the cod, remove the bones, then boil it in plenty of water with the garlic and parsley for 20–30 minutes, until tender.

Drain the fish, place it in a bowl and, using a wooden spoon, squash it into a paste with plenty of olive oil and black pepper.

Spread it over slices of bread and serve.

BACCALA E CECI

SALT COD WITH CHICKPEAS

My uncle Nando used to love anything made with chickpeas, so my aunt used to cook this dish especially for him.

Serves 4

600g/1lb 5 oz salt cod
200g/7oz chickpeas
salt

To serve:
best-quality extra-virgin olive oil
freshly ground black pepper

Soak the salt cod overnight, in several changes of water. Soak the chickpeas overnight.

Cook the chickpeas in plenty of slightly salted water for about 35 minutes.

Clean the cod, cut it into chunks and cook it in boiling water for approximately 10 minutes.

Drain the fish, place it on a warmed platter and garnish with the chickpeas. Dress it with best-quality olive oil and freshly ground black pepper.

Tip:
Canned chickpeas, borlotti beans or cannellini beans can be used for this dish, but only if they have been canned in water. Drain them and rinse in warm water. Boil for 1 minute and then drain.

BACCALA ALLA FIORENTINA

FLORENTINE SALT COD

This, along with Baccala Bianco (see page 150) is the most common salt cod dish of all. Tuscans love to have something to dip their bread into, and this sauce is perfect.

Serves 4

600g/1lb 5oz salt cod
90ml/3fl oz/scant ½ cup olive oil
1 garlic clove
1 onion, chopped
500g/1lb 2oz fresh ripe tomatoes, skinned and roughly chopped
plain (all-purpose) white flour for coating
1 tbsp chopped fresh parsley
freshly ground black pepper

Soak the salt cod overnight, in several changes of water.

Rinse the fish and trim to remove the fin, bones and skin. Cut it into chunks and pat dry with a clean teatowel or kitchen paper.

Heat a little oil in a saucepan and sauté the garlic and onion for a few minutes. Remove the garlic when golden brown and add the tomatoes. Season with pepper and simmer for about 15 minutes.

Meanwhile, coat the chunks of fish in flour and fry them in a pan with a little olive oil. When golden on both sides, lift them out and arrange them in a lightly oiled flameproof earthenware or other heavy-based casserole.

Sieve the tomato sauce and pour it over the fish. Simmer over a low heat for 6–7 minutes. Sprinkle with parsley and serve immediately.

ANGUILLA MARINATA

MARINATED EEL

This is one eel dish that my father would eat, even though it broke his rule of not eating anything that didn't look like a fish. Whenever I caught an eel, this is what my mother would make. The eel needs to marinate for 48 hours before serving.

Serves 4

1 eel, weighing about 1kg/2lb
bran, for rubbing the eel
plain (all-purpose) white flour for coating
olive oil for frying
1 litre/1¾ pints/4¾ cups red-wine vinegar
2 garlic cloves
1 fresh rosemary sprig
1 small piece of dried red chilli
salt and black peppercorns

Do not skin the eel, but rub it in bran to make it less slippery. Gut it, remove the fins and wash it in plenty of water. Cut it into pieces about 6cm/2½ inches long. Dry the pieces and coat them in flour.

Heat the oil in a frying-pan (skillet) and fry the pieces of eel. When golden on both sides, drain and place in a large bowl.

Meanwhile, simmer the vinegar with the garlic, rosemary, chilli and a few peppercorns for about 30 minutes. Leave this marinade to cool and, when barely warm, pour over the eel. Leave for 48 hours to marinate.

TRIGLIE ALLA LIVORNESE

LIVORNESE RED MULLET

We would only have this delicious dish during the summer months, when fresh, ripe tomatoes were available.

Serves 4

12 small red mullet or red snapper
plain (all-purpose) white flour for coating
olive oil for frying
salt
Italian parsley leaves to garnish

For the tomato sauce:
90ml/3fl oz/scant ½ cup olive oil
3 garlic cloves, crushed
1 heaped tbsp chopped fresh parsley
500g/1lb 2oz fresh ripe tomatoes, skinned and roughly chopped
salt and freshly ground black pepper

Clean and gut the fish and wash them in running water. Shake off excess water and dry with a clean teatowel.

To make the tomato sauce: heat the olive oil in a saucepan and sauté the garlic and parsley. Add the tomatoes, season with salt and pepper and simmer for about 20 minutes. Sieve the sauce.

Meanwhile, coat the fish in flour. Put a little oil in a frying-pan (skillet) and fry the fish until golden on both sides. Drain them and sprinkle with salt. Arrange them in a large, oiled, flameproof casserole and cover them with tomato sauce.

Simmer for 5 minutes, then serve, garnished with parsley.

TRIGLIE ALLA MAREMMANA

MAREMMA-STYLE RED MULLET

Maremma is a region of Southern Tuscany which is usually associated with ham and cheese. My father used to love this dish.

Serves 4

800g/1lb 12oz red mullet
100g/4oz prosciutto crudo (raw cured ham), finely minced (ground)
20g/¾oz/1 tbsp butter
175ml/6fl oz/¾ cup dry white wine
90ml/3fl oz/scant ½ cup olive oil
juice of ½ lemon
1 garlic clove, finely chopped
salt and freshly ground black pepper
fresh white breadcrumbs for coating

Clean and gut the red mullet, wash them in plenty of running water and leave to dry for a few minutes.

Stuff the fish with prosciutto and a knob of butter and place them in a bowl.

Make a marinade with the wine, olive oil, lemon juice, garlic and a pinch of salt and pepper and pour it over the fish. Leave for a couple of hours, turning the fish over a few times.

Preheat the oven to 180°C/350°F/Gas Mark 4. Coat the red mullet in breadcrumbs and arrange them in a single layer in an oiled ovenproof dish. Sprinkle with 2 tbsp of the marinade and bake for 20–25 minutes, sprinkling with more of the marinade from time to time, to prevent the fish from drying out.

Serve straight from the dish.

BIANCHETTI ALLA VERSIGLIESE

LIVORNESE WHITEBAIT

This is another Versiglian dish, from the seaside of Tuscany. Bianchetti are actually a little bigger than the whitebait you can buy in Britain. If there was any left over, my mother would add a little tomato sauce and put it on top of pasta the following day.

Serves 4

400g/14oz whitebait
90ml/3fl oz/scant ½ cup olive oil
1 onion, finely chopped
2 eggs
juice of 1 lemon
salt and freshly ground black pepper

Rinse the whitebait.

Put some oil in a flameproof casserole or frying-pan (skillet) and fry the onion until soft. Add the whitebait and cook for about 2 minutes, stirring all the time.

Beat the eggs with a pinch of salt, pepper and half the lemon juice. Pour into the pan. Keep stirring until the eggs have set. Sprinkle with the remaining lemon juice and serve immediately.

TORTA DI ACCIUGHE

ANCHOVY CAKE

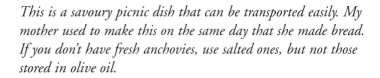

This is a savoury picnic dish that can be transported easily. My mother used to make this on the same day that she made bread. If you don't have fresh anchovies, use salted ones, but not those stored in olive oil.

Serves 4

handful of salted anchovies
250g/9oz onions, thinly sliced
1 tbsp chopped fresh parsley
salt and grated nutmeg
olive oil

For the dough:
300g/11oz/2 cups plain (all-purpose) white flour
2 eggs
salt
30g/1oz/2 tbsp butter, softened

To make the dough: tip the flour on to a work surface and knead it together with the eggs, a pinch of salt and the butter. When it is well kneaded, put the dough in a warm place for 30 minutes, covered with a clean cloth.

Meanwhile, rinse the anchovies and leave them to dry for several minutes. Preheat the oven to 220°C/425°F/Gas Mark 7.

Put the dough on a floured work surface, divide it in half and roll out each half quite thickly. Line the bottom and sides of an oiled 25cm/10-inch cake tin (pan) with one half of the dough.

Arrange the filling ingredients on the dough in this order: onions, anchovies, parsley, a pinch of salt and nutmeg and a sprinkling of olive oil.

Cover with the other half of the dough, pressing the edges carefully together all the way round so that the pie is thoroughly sealed. Bake for about 25 minutes or until the top is golden brown in colour.

PESCE SPADA IN UMIDO

SWORDFISH IN TOMATO SAUCE

WITH POTATOES

My wife, Letizia, gave me this recipe. Swordfish is normally cooked like this, in a stew. People have started to grill it only in the last few years because of the new trend to make food plain and simple.

Serves 4

600g/1lb 5oz swordfish steaks
175ml/6fl oz/¾ cup olive oil
1 onion, finely chopped
1 carrot, finely chopped
handful of finely chopped fresh parsley
500g/1lb 2oz fresh ripe tomatoes, skinned, de-seeded and puréed
250g/9oz potatoes, peeled and cut into medium-size pieces
90ml/3fl oz/scant ½ cup *vin santo* (Tuscan dessert wine)
salt and freshly ground black pepper

Wash the swordfish steaks and cut them into chunks.

Put half the the oil in a saucepan and sauté the onion, carrot and parsley for a few minutes. Add the tomatoes and simmer for about 20 minutes.

Add the potatoes and simmer for 1 hour.

Put the remaining oil in a flameproof casserole and brown the fish chunks. Add to the tomato sauce and potatoes, cover and simmer for 25 minutes, adding a little hot water whenever the dish seems to be drying out.

Sprinkle with vin santo, season and cook for a further 5 minutes.

SGOMBRO AL LIMONE CON OLIVE

BAKED MACKEREL WITH LEMON JUICE

Even in Italy, mackerel is a cheap fish, although it is not as cheap as in Britain. In Tuscany, it is known as 'poor man's tuna fish'. My mother would sometimes buy mackerel instead of tuna – I prefer it to tuna, so I was never disappointed.

Serves 4

2 mackerel, filleted
5 lemons
4 tbsp olive oil
100g/4oz large black Greek olives
20 fresh Italian parsley sprigs
salt and freshly ground black pepper
lemon slices and Italian parsley leaves to garnish

Wash the fish carefully under cold running water. Very lightly oil a glass baking dish and place the fish in the dish.

Remove the zest of the lemons with a zester and chop it very finely. Squeeze the juice of the lemons into a bowl, add salt and pepper and mix very well. Pour over the fish and cover the dish with cling film (plastic wrap). Refrigerate overnight.

Preheat the oven to 200°C/400°F/Gas Mark 6. Remove and discard all but 2 tbsp of the lemon juice and pour the oil all over the fish. Bake for 15 minutes.

As the fish is cooking, finely chop the olives and parsley together. Add the lemon zest and mix very well. Sprinkle this mixture over the mackerel and serve garnished with lemon slices and parsley leaves.

TONNO UBRIACO

'DRUNKEN' TUNA FISH

Tuna is a very common fish in Tuscany. I have used Chianti in this recipe, but you can use any red wine.

Serves 4

90ml/3fl oz/scant ½ cup olive oil
1 garlic clove
1 onion, sliced
1 tbsp chopped fresh parsley
4 fresh tuna steaks
1 tbsp plain (all-purpose) white flour
175ml/6fl oz/¾ cup Chianti wine
salt and freshly ground black pepper

Put the oil in a frying-pan (skillet) and sauté the garlic, onion and parsley for a few minutes.

When the garlic has turned golden, remove it. Arrange the fish steaks in the pan and cook until done, about 1 minute on each side. Season with salt and pepper and sprinkle the flour into the pan, to thicken the cooking juices. After 2 minutes, stir in the wine.

Cook for a further 5 minutes and serve.

TROTE ALLA MUGNAIA

MILLER'S TROUT

Trout is used in many Tuscan recipes since it is so readily available. It can be found in our ponds as well as in the man-made lakes of the Apennine mountains. Sometimes my family and I would go on an excursion into the countryside. My sister would pick wildflowers and I would try and catch trout; you are really supposed to use a hook, but I always used a net.

Serves 4

4 trout, weighing around 250g/9oz each, cleaned and gutted
90ml/3fl oz/scant ½ cup olive oil
2 garlic cloves, chopped
plain (all-purpose) white flour for coating
salt
90ml/3fl oz/scant ½ cup dry white wine
1 tbsp chopped fresh parsley to garnish

Rinse and dry the trout.

Put the oil in a large frying-pan (skillet) and sauté the garlic. Coat the trout in flour and put them in the pan. Fry, turning the fish once, for about 5 minutes on each side.

Season with salt, sprinkle with the wine and, when this has evaporated, serve garnished with parsley.

PESCIOLINI FRITTI

DEEP-FRIED MIXED FISH

We used to eat this dish quite often during the summer months with a salad; it is one of the most common deep-fried fish dishes in Tuscany.

Serves 4

600g/1lb 5oz small river or sea fish
plain (all-purpose) white flour for coating
olive oil for deep- or shallow-frying
salt
lemon wedges to garnish

Wash the fish in plenty of water and leave to drain thoroughly.

Coat the fish in flour.

Heat the oil for frying until it is very hot. Deep-fry the fish for 3 minutes or shallow-fry for 4 minutes. When they are golden and crunchy, lift from the oil and place on kitchen paper to drain.

Sprinkle with salt and serve with lemon wedges.

CACCIUCCO

TRADITIONAL TUSCAN FISH STEW

Serves 4

1.5kg/3lb mixed fish and seafood, e.g. sole,
   razor, cuttlefish, squid, prawns and mussels
olive oil
1 onion, chopped
1 tbsp chopped fresh parsley
3 garlic cloves
1 small piece of dried red chilli
300g/11oz fresh ripe tomatoes, skinned and
   roughly chopped
350ml/12fl oz dry white wine
salt and freshly ground black pepper

To serve:
4 slices of stale country-style bread
1 garlic clove, halved

*This is a very well-known soup, which could also be called
'Mother's fish stew', as it is cooked in homes all over Tuscany
and evokes memories of home-cooking for all Tuscans. It is as
ubiquitous as the French* bouillabaisse; *in fact, some say that the
the French borrowed this recipe, without the tomatoes, for their
dish. I am pleased to give you the Tuscan recipe.*

Clean and gut the fish, reserving the heads. Wash the fish and
cut into chunks, keeping the different fish apart.

Wash the fish heads and set aside.

Put some oil in an earthenware or other flameproof casserole
and sauté the onion and parsley until soft.

Meanwhile, crush the garlic with a pestle and mortar and mix
it with the chilli and mixed fish and seafood. Add this mixture to
the onion and parsley. Fry for around 4 minutes; then lift the fish
out and arrange it on a plate, keeping it warm in some sauce or
hot water, or they will become tough.

Add the tomatoes to the pan and cook for a further 10 minutes.
Add the fish heads, sprinkle with the wine and season with salt
and pepper. Cook for 30 minutes, adding hot water if the dish is
drying out.

Sieve the mixture into a clean saucepan, or liquidize or process
it. Dilute with enough hot water to produce a not-too-thick purée
and return to the boil. As soon as it boils, add the fish, including
the squid and cuttlefish; simmer for around 20 minutes.

Meanwhile, toast the bread, rub it with the cut surface of the
garlic and place the slices at the bottom of the serving dishes.
Spoon the fish on top and serve at once.

RICE

ITALY TODAY IS WELL KNOWN FOR PIZZA AND PASTA, BUT WE MUST ALSO MENTION RICE, WHICH HAS BEEN USED IN ITALY FOR 1000 YEARS: IT WAS INTRODUCED BY VENETIAN MERCHANTS AT THE END OF THE TENTH CENTURY.

The rice we use in Italy to make risotto is called 'Japonica Crystalline' and, after China, we are the biggest producers of this type of rice. Italy has 475,000 hectares (1,173,750 acres) of land producing rice, and we produce far more rice than wheat, which is why most of our pasta flour (durum flour) is imported from Canada.

To make a hot risotto, you must use *arborio* rice, which grows in Italy and is white, with short, fat grains, like pudding rice. If you want to make a rice salad, use steamed Chinese rice. Another famous Italian rice is called *avorio*, because of its ivory colour. This can be oven-baked, because the grains never stick together. Put it in an ovenproof dish with a chopped onion, a couple of bay leaves and enough water to cover the rice plus 2.5cm/1 inch, for 25 minutes. You should be able to see each grain of rice when it is cooked. Serve it with sauce as a main course or use it to make a rice salad. You can use *avorio* rice to make risotto, but only with a creamy type of sauce. Both of these rices are varieties of 'Japonica Crystalline'.

Most risotti, no matter what ingredients are used, have the same base: a *soffrito* (derived from 'to fry gently') of finely chopped onions, carrots and celery, or any one or combination of two of these, fried in butter or olive oil. You need to cook risotto in a fairly heavy-based frying-pan (skillet) or a shallow, heavy, flameproof casserole, which distributes heat evenly and so prevents the risotto from sticking on the bottom as it cooks.

Sauté the onions (and carrots and celery) until the onions are translucent, then add the rice. Stir the rice to make sure all the grains have been coated in oil or butter, so they are shiny. Add water or stock – beef, chicken or vegetable according to the other ingredients – a ladleful at a time and wait for the first addition to be absorbed by the rice before adding any more. Stir the risotto all the time as it cooks, to stop it from sticking to the pan and to make it more creamy. The end result should be moist, but exactly how solid or liquid you make the risotto, and exactly how soft the rice grains are, is a matter of personal taste.

RISO E CASTAGNE

RISOTTO WITH CHESTNUTS

We used to eat this risotto on 2 November for Remembrance Day, when the hills are full of sweet chestnuts.

Serves 4

300g/11oz dried chestnuts
500ml/17fl oz/2¼ cups milk
salt and grated nutmeg
150g/5oz/¾ cup risotto rice, preferably Italian arborio

Soak the chestnuts overnight in cold water.

When ready to use, peel off the skins and boil the chestnuts in plenty of salted water for 25 minutes.

Once the chestnuts are cooked, lift them with a slotted spoon into a bowl and keep warm.

Pour the milk into the chestnut cooking water, sprinkle with nutmeg and bring to the boil. (You should have about 1.2 litres/2 pints/5 cups, so add more milk or water if necessary.)

Tip the rice into a flameproof casserole dish. Add a couple of ladlefuls of the chestnut liquid and stir. Cook for 15 minutes, stirring frequently and adding more liquid in batches as the rice dries out.

Add the chestnuts and cook for a further 5 minutes. Serve piping hot.

RISOTTA CON LE SALSICCE

RISOTTO WITH SAUSAGE SAUCE

This recipe comes from a lady called Adelide, who was the wife of the tailor in my village. As we didn't eat risotto at home all that often, she used to cook this for me.

Serves 4

200g/7oz *salsicce* (Italian sausages)
90ml/3fl oz/scant ½ cup olive oil
1 onion, sliced
300g/11oz ripe tomatoes, skinned, de-seeded and chopped
about 1.2 litres/2 pints/5 cups stock, brought to the boil
300g/11oz/1½ cups risotto rice, preferably Italian arborio
salt and freshly ground black pepper
2 tbsp grated parmesan cheese, to serve

Skin and mince (grind) the sausages.

Heat the oil in a shallow, flameproof casserole or heavy-based frying-pan (skillet), add the onion and cook until softened.

Add the sausages and cook until browned. Then add the tomatoes, season with salt and pepper and simmer for 10 minutes, sprinkling with a little hot stock if necessary to prevent the tomatoes from drying out.

Add the rice, stir thoroughly and cover to the surface with very hot stock, then cook, adding more stock as the rice absorbs the liquid. You may not need all the stock.

Check the seasoning and then stir in the parmesan before serving.

POLPETTINE DI RISO AL SUGO

RICE DUMPLINGS WITH MEAT SAUCE

Serves 6

For the rice balls:
300g/11oz/1½ cups risotto rice, preferably
    Italian arborio
about 1.2 litres/2 pints/5 cups milk
150g/5oz leftover boiled or roasted meat,
    minced (ground)
50g/2oz/½ cup grated parmesan cheese
handful of chopped fresh marjoram and parsley
soft part of a small bread roll, soaked in milk
    and squeezed dry
1 egg, beaten
salt, freshly ground black pepper and grated
    nutmeg
Ragu di Carne alla Pistoiese (page 178) or
    bolognese sauce, made with less meat
    and more tomatoes, or any tomato sauce
    (for example, page 181), to serve

To finish:
plain (all-purpose) white flour for coating
1 egg, beaten with salt and pepper
fresh white breadcrumbs for coating
olive oil for frying

This is a snack which you will see in wine and snack bars in Italy. It is eaten at any time, often with a glass of wine. As a boy, I used to take them to school in a little box to eat at breaktime.

Cook the rice in the milk until soft. Drain off any excess milk.

Put the rice into a bowl and add the minced (ground) meat, parmesan, marjoram, parsley, the moist bread, egg and a pinch each of salt, pepper and nutmeg. Mix all the ingredients together and shape into balls.

Coat the rice balls in flour, dip them in the beaten egg, and then coat them in the breadcrumbs.

Heat the oil in a frying-pan (skillet) and fry the rice balls until golden. Drain them on kitchen paper.

Reheat the sauce in a flameproof casserole or large saucepan. Put the rice balls in the sauce and cook for a few minutes.

Serve straight from the casserole or saucepan.

RISOTTO CON FAGIOLI

RISOTTO WITH CANNELLINI BEANS

Serves 4

225g/8oz/1 cup dried cannellini beans
1.2 litres/2 pints/5 cups cold water
1 large garlic clove
2 fresh or dry sage leaves
250g/9oz/1¼ cups cups risotto rice, preferably
   Italian arborio
salt and freshly ground black pepper
fresh basil leaves, to serve

For the sauce:
100g/4oz pancetta or prosciutto or bacon
5 tbsp olive oil
2 red onions, coarsely chopped
2 carrots, coarsely chopped
1 celery stick, coarsely chopped
1 large garlic clove, chopped
10 fresh Italian parsley sprigs, chopped
10 fresh basil leaves, chopped
salt, pepper and a large pinch of hot red
   pepper flakes
750g/1lb 10oz very ripe tomatoes or canned
   tomatoes

This is a fantastic dish – even when eaten the following day with some extra virgin olive oil. I don't serve it in my restaurant because it really is very filling. It's wholesome and good and something I make for a special treat.

Soak the beans in cold water overnight.

The next day, drain the beans and put them in a stockpot, along with the water, garlic and sage leaves. Bring to the boil over a medium heat, then lower the heat and simmer for about 45 minutes, until the beans are cooked but still firm.

Drain the beans, saving the water, and sprinkle with salt and pepper. Cover the bowl until needed.

To make the sauce
Cut the pancetta or prosciutto or bacon into tiny pieces.

Heat the oil in a large flameproof casserole over a low heat, then add the onions, carrots, celery, garlic, herbs and bacon. Sauté for 20 minutes, stirring every so often with a wooden spoon.

Season with salt and pepper and the hot red pepper flakes.

If using fresh tomatoes, blanch and remove the skins and seeds, and add them to the casserole. If using canned tomatoes, purée them in a food processor and pour into the casserole. Stir well and simmer for 30 minutes more.

When the sauce is ready, take 500ml/16fl oz/2 cups of it and pour it over the beans.

To make the risotto
Measure the reserved cooking water from the beans and add enough cold water to yield about 1 litre/1¾ pints/4 cups of liquid. Bring to the boil.

Add the rice to the remaining sauce in the casserole and sauté over medium heat for 4 minutes, stirring constantly with a wooden spoon. Start adding the boiling liquid, 125ml/4fl oz/ ½ cup at a time, stirring constantly. Add more liquid only when the previous ½ cup has been completely absorbed.

When all the liquid is incorporated and the rice is cooked (but is still *al dente,* as risotto should be), add the beans, stirring constantly. Taste for salt and pepper while continuing to stir.

Transfer the risotto to a warmed serving platter and serve immediately, with the basil leaves.

RISOTTO AL BASILICO

RISOTTO WITH BASIL SAUCE

My mother used to make this in the summer. We liked it so much that my mother always used to make a little bit extra so that we could eat it cold the next day with some more olive oil and basil.

Serves 4

1.6 litres/2¾ pints/7 cups home-made light chicken stock
30 fresh basil leaves
75g/3oz/½ cup butter
1 tbsp olive oil
1 large onion, finely chopped
375g/13oz/2 cups risotto rice, preferably Italian arborio
salt and freshly ground black pepper

To finish:
30 fresh basil leaves
25g/1oz/2 tbsp unsalted butter
4 tbsp grated parmesan cheese, plus extra to serve

Bring the stock, with the basil leaves, to the boil over a medium heat, then lower the heat and simmer for 15 minutes. The broth will reduce to about 1.5 litres/2³/₄ pints/6 cups.

Put the butter and oil in a medium-sized flameproof casserole over a medium heat until the butter melts. Add the onion and sauté for 5 minutes or until the onion is translucent. Add the rice and sauté for 4 minutes, stirring constantly with a wooden spoon.

Discard the basil leaves from the boiling stock. Start adding the boiling liquid to the rice, 125ml/4fl oz/¹/₂ cup at a time, stirring constantly with a wooden spoon. Add more stock only when the previous ¹/₂ cup has been completely absorbed.

When the stock is all used up, the risotto should be ready and the grains cooked *al dente*. Season with salt and pepper.

Immediately, finely chop the basil (or have somebody else do it for you, because the basil must be chopped at the last minute while you are busy stirring the risotto).

Remove the casserole from the heat, add the basil, butter and parmesan, and mix very well with a wooden spoon. Serve hot, with additional grated parmesan.

INSALATA DI RISO CON OLIVE

RICE AND OLIVE SALAD

We used to eat this salad on summer evenings, sitting outside in the courtyard. I remember watching the sun go down as we ate, and the swallows would be chasing each other in the sky.

Serves 4

200g/7oz/generous 1 cup risotto rice, preferably Italian arborio
8 tbsp olive oil
100g/4oz bacon, cut into strips
2 garlic cloves
pinch of chilli powder
2 slices of white bread, soaked in water and squeezed out
1 tbsp wine vinegar
450g/1lb canned cannellini beans, drained and rinsed
100g/4oz lean prosciutto or ham, chopped
50g/2oz canned anchovy fillets, drained
10 large green olives, halved and pitted
12 fresh parsley sprigs, chopped
pinch of chopped fresh marjoram
few fresh basil leaves (optional), chopped
salt and freshly ground black pepper

Boil the rice in salted water until tender; drain and rinse under cold running water.

While the rice is cooking, heat 1 tbsp of oil in a frying-pan (skillet) and sauté the strips of bacon.

In a small bowl, crush the garlic with the chilli powder, add the bread, the rest of the oil, the vinegar, salt and pepper. Mix well to make a dressing.

In a salad bowl, combine the cooked rice, the beans, ham, anchovy fillets, olives and the bacon strips. Add some of the dressing, mix thoroughly, and then garnish the salad with parsley, marjoram and basil.

RISOTTO ALLA CONTADINA

FARMHOUSE RISOTTO

A neighbour of mine gave me this recipe, which is a very rustic type of risotto. You can vary the vegetables you use, if you like.

Serves 4

3 tbsp olive oil
50g/2oz lard
1 onion, finely chopped
1 carrot, finely chopped
1 celery stick, finely chopped
fresh basil leaves
300g/11oz potatoes, diced
150g/5oz courgettes (zucchini), diced
300g/11oz ripe tomatoes, skinned, de-seeded and puréed
about 1.2 litres/2 pints/5 cups chicken stock, brought to the boil
300g/11oz fresh peas, shelled
300g/11oz/1½ cups risotto rice, preferably Italian arborio
salt and freshly ground black pepper
grated parmesan cheese, to serve

In a saucepan, heat the oil and lard and sauté the onion, carrot, celery and basil until the onion is translucent. Add the potatoes, courgettes (zucchini) and tomatoes, and stir, making sure that they are thoroughly mixed. Season to taste with salt and pepper and simmer for about 20 minutes, adding a little hot stock from time to time, if necessary.

Add the peas and cook for about 2 minutes, then add the rice. Stir thoroughly and add enough boiling stock to cover the surface of the rice. Cook for 18–19 minutes, adding more stock as it dries out. Check the seasoning – it should be well seasoned – and serve, passing the grated parmesan separately.

RISOTTO CON CARCIOFI

RISOTTO WITH BABY ARTICHOKES

Risotto in Italy was more commonly eaten in winter. Lately, it has become a dish that we eat all year round. This artichoke risotto was a favourite dish of my father's. It's really very good!

Serves 4

6 baby globe artichokes
juice of 1 lemon
100g/4oz prosciutto crudo (raw cured ham)
1 tbsp olive oil (optional)
2 garlic cloves
1 tbsp chopped fresh parsley
about 1.2 litres/2 pints/5 cups vegetable stock, brought to the boil
300g/11oz/1½ cups risotto rice, preferably Italian arborio
salt and freshly ground black pepper
grated parmesan cheese, to serve

Clean the artichokes by removing the hard outer leaves and the sharp tips; wash and soak them in a basin of cold water to which you have added the lemon juice, to prevent them from discolouring. Leave to drain, and then cut them into segments.

Sauté the prosciutto in a large earthenware or other heavy-based, flameproof casserole, with the garlic and parsley, adding the oil if necessary to prevent it from sticking.

Remove the garlic when browned and, after a few minutes, stir in the artichokes. Cook for a few more minutes and then pour in half a ladleful of boiling stock. Cook for 10 minutes.

Add the rice, season and cover to the surface with boiling stock. Cook over a low heat, stirring frequently and adding more stock as it is absorbed by the rice, until the rice is cooked, but still *al dente*, which will probably take about 25 minutes.

Stir in a handful of grated parmesan just before serving.

SAUCES

VERY RARELY DO WE TUSCANS MAKE A SPECIAL SAUCE FOR
PASTA. INSTEAD, WHEN WE MAKE STEW FROM MEAT,
VEGETABLES OR FISH, WE USUALLY MAKE SOME EXTRA TO PUT
ON PASTA, SO WE END UP WITH TWO DISHES: OUR MAIN
COURSE OF STEW AS WELL AS PASTA AND SAUCE AS A STARTER.
HOWEVER, I HAVE GIVEN YOU HERE A FEW RECIPES FOR SAUCES
SPECIALLY MADE FOR PASTA.

SALSA BIANCA

BÉCHAMEL SAUCE

This is the sauce we use to make lasagne with – indeed, if I remember correctly, it was only ever used for lasagne.

Makes about 1.2 litres/2 pints/5 cups

125g/4oz/½ cup butter
½ onion, very finely chopped
8 tbsp plain (all-purpose) white flour
1.2 litres/2 pints/5 cups milk
grated nutmeg
salt and freshly ground black pepper
600ml/1 pint/2½ cups double (heavy) cream (optional)

Melt the butter in a heavy-based saucepan, stir in the onion and sauté until soft. Add the flour and cook, stirring, over a low heat, for 2–3 minutes. Pour in all the milk, whisking constantly to blend the mixture smoothly. Increase the heat and continue whisking until the sauce comes to the boil. Add the nutmeg and a pinch of salt.

Reduce the heat and simmer for at least 45 minutes, stirring every so often to prevent the sauce from sticking to the bottom of the pan.

If you want to keep the sauce for more than 2 or 3 hours, strain it though a sieve into another saucepan. Whisk in the cream, to give the same consistency, over a low heat. This will prevent a skin from forming on the surface.

Season with salt and pepper, if necessary, before using.

SALSA DI CARCIOFI PER LA PASTA

ARTICHOKE SAUCE

This sauce is particularly suitable for egg pasta. When artichokes are very small, they are ideal for a dish like this, because you can't really do more than chop them up and use them in a sauce.

Serves 6

10 small globe artichokes
4 tbsp olive oil
1 onion, finely chopped
2 garlic cloves, crushed
150g/5oz/1 cup plain (all-purpose) white flour
200g/7oz/1¾ cups grated parmesan cheese
salt and freshly ground black pepper

Clean the artichokes and discard the hard parts. Cut each one in quarters.

Heat the oil in a frying-pan (skillet) and sauté the onion and garlic until golden.

Meanwhile, coat the artichokes in flour. Add to the frying-pan (skillet), with salt, pepper and a little water if the sauce looks too dry. Cover and cook until the artichokes are tender, about 20–30 minutes, depending on the age of the artichokes.

Add the parmesan and let the sauce stand for 10 minutes before serving.

SALSA FEGATINI DI POLLO

CHICKEN LIVER SAUCE

This sauce is suitable for egg pasta, such as tagliatelle or fettucine. Egg pasta does not take on too much of the strong flavour of the chicken livers and so blends well with the sauce.

Serves 4

400g/14oz chicken livers
6 tbsp olive oil
2 garlic cloves, squashed
1 large onion, finely chopped
4 bay leaves
grated nutmeg
4 tbsp red wine
1 tbsp tomato purée (paste), diluted in 3 tbsp water
100g/4oz/1 cup grated pecorino or parmesan cheese (pecorino is best)
salt and freshly ground black pepper

Cut the chicken livers into small pieces.

Heat the oil and fry the garlic and onion for 5 minutes or until they begin to brown. Remove the garlic. Add the chicken livers and bay leaves and fry gently for 15 minutes over a low heat.

Add a little nutmeg, then add the red wine. Let the alcohol evaporate. Add the diluted tomato purée (paste) to the liver and stir. At this stage, you may add more water to bring the sauce to a smooth consistency. Season to taste with salt and pepper.

Add the cheese to the sauce just before serving.

RAGU DI CARNE ALLA PISTOIESE

PISTOIESE MEAT SAUCE

Pistoia is the town nearest to Bologna in Tuscany and this sauce is very similar to a bolognese sauce. It is prepared with different herbs, but the procedure is the same. It may seem fiddly to remove the meat from the sauce and mince (grind) it, but it is worth doing for a really rich sauce.

Serves 6

20g/¾ oz dried porcini mushrooms
90ml/3fl oz/scant ½ cup olive oil
1 onion, finely chopped
1 carrot, finely chopped
1 celery stick, finely chopped
1 tbsp chopped fresh basil
1 tbsp chopped fresh parsley
500g/1lb 2oz braising or stewing steak
175ml/6fl oz/¾ cup red wine
350g/12oz ripe tomatoes, skinned, de-seeded and puréed
beef stock
salt and freshly ground black pepper

Soak the porcini in warm water for about 15 minutes. Drain, keeping the mushroom water.

Heat the oil and fry the onion, carrot, celery, basil and parsley, until the onion is soft and translucent.

Add the beef and stir to brown all over. When it is well browned, season with salt and pepper and pour in the red wine. Simmer until almost dry and then add the tomatoes and the mushrooms. Simmer the sauce for 40 minutes adding, when necessary, first the mushroom water and then the hot stock, to prevent the sauce from drying out.

Remove the meat and mince (grind) it. Then return it to the saucepan and cook for a further 20 minutes.

SALSA AL DRAGONCELLO

TARRAGON SAUCE

My grandmother used to love tarragon. In fact, she liked it so much that she would put it inside her linen drawer so that her clean sheets would smell nice. She also made this sauce, which is ideal with boiled meats.

Serves 4

handful of fresh tarragon leaves
4 garlic cloves
50g/2oz white bread, crust removed
270ml/9fl oz/generous 1 cup wine vinegar
salt
about 4 tbsp best-quality extra-virgin olive oil

Chop the tarragon leaves with the garlic and transfer to a bowl.

Soak the bread in the vinegar, squeeze it dry, then mix it with the tarragon and garlic. Season with very little salt and push through a fine sieve.

Using a wooden spoon, beat enough olive oil into the mixture to obtain a smooth sauce.

SUGO DI POMODORO CASALINGA

COUNTRY-STYLE TOMATO SAUCE

Every housewife will make this sauce in Tuscany. It is, of course, excellent on pasta.

Serves 4–6

90ml/3fl oz/scant ½ cup olive oil
1 carrot, finely chopped
1 onion, finely chopped
1 celery stick, finely chopped
finely chopped fresh basil and parsley
500g/1lb 2oz fresh ripe tomatoes, skinned, de-seeded and puréed, or canned, peeled tomatoes
salt and freshly ground black pepper

Heat the oil and fry the carrot, onion, celery and herbs until the onion is soft and translucent. Add salt, pepper and the tomatoes.

Simmer over a low heat for at least 20 minutes, adding a little water from time to time. It should be well reduced before serving.

SALSA DI BROCCOLI

BROCCOLI SAUCE

This is good for all types of short dried pasta, such as rigatoni or fusilli. Mamma used to make this with rigatoni, and sometimes she would serve it on its own as a vegetable dish.

Serves 4

500g/1lb 2oz fresh broccoli
6 tbsp olive oil
2 garlic cloves, squashed
6 tbsp water
salt and freshly ground black pepper
100g/4oz/1 cup grated parmesan cheese, to serve

Chop the broccoli very finely.

Heat the oil with the garlic (the garlic can be removed afterwards, if desired). When the garlic is brown, add the broccoli and water.

Cover and cook for at least 20 minutes, stirring every 5 minutes, until the broccoli is softened and smoothed by the stirring action.

Season with salt and pepper to taste. Add the cheese and stir before serving.

SALSA CRUDA

SUMMER SAUCE

This sauce is suitable for spaghetti or linguine. It is not cooked.

Serves 4

4 ripe tomatoes
2 mozzarella cheeses
20 fresh basil leaves
4 sun-dried tomatoes
8 tbsp best-quality extra-virgin olive oil
salt and freshly ground black pepper

Peel the tomatoes and de-seed them. Chop the flesh into little cubes of about 1 cm/¹/₂-inch square.

Chop the mozzarella into the same sized cubes. Tear the basil leaves with your hands, or chop them, to the same size. Chop the sun-dried tomatoes.

Place all the ingredients in a glass bowl. Add olive oil, and salt and pepper to taste.

Put the cooked pasta into the sauce and toss.

SALSA DI PISELLI

PEA SAUCE

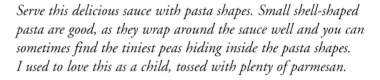

Serve this delicious sauce with pasta shapes. Small shell-shaped pasta are good, as they wrap around the sauce well and you can sometimes find the tiniest peas hiding inside the pasta shapes. I used to love this as a child, tossed with plenty of parmesan.

Serves 4

2 tbsp olive oil
100g/4oz streaky bacon, finely chopped
300g/11oz onions, finely chopped
1 leek, trimmed and very finely chopped
300g/11oz frozen petits pois
salt and freshly ground black pepper
200g/7oz/1¾ cups grated parmesan cheese, to serve

In a medium saucepan, heat the olive oil and fry the bacon for 5 minutes on a high heat.

Add the onions and leek, cover and cook until soft, about 15 minutes on a medium heat.

Add the peas, and salt and pepper to taste. Cook for another 20 minutes or until the sauce is fairly dry.

Add the parmesan cheese and stir well.

SALSA DI POMODORO

PLAIN TOMATO SAUCE

This sauce was made on a Monday or a Tuesday. When we had a fridge after the war, we were able to keep it for three or four days. You must take it out of the fridge an hour before you use it, but don't heat it up – just put it on top of the hot pasta, toss well, sprinkle with some fresh basil and it will be perfect. One day, I asked my mother why we must never reheat this sauce, and she told me that in order to taste the lovely flavour of the tomatoes, it must be served at room temperature – hot tomatoes, you see, have no flavour.

Serves 6–8

2kg/4lb 8 oz ripe, but not over-ripe, fresh tomatoes
2 onions, sliced
4 garlic cloves, crushed
fresh basil leaves
90ml/3fl oz/scant ½ cup best-quality extra-virgin olive oil

Wash the tomatoes and chop each one into four. Place all the tomatoes in a large saucepan.

Put the onions and garlic in the saucepan, bring to the boil and simmer for 25–30 minutes. If the tomatoes are producing too much water, simmer for a further 30 minutes.

Then pass the whole lot through a strainer or mouli-legumes, to remove the tomato seeds and skin.

Put the sauce into a bowl and dress the top with fresh basil leaves. Add the extra-virgin olive oil and leave for 1–2 hours at room temperature. Never put this sauce hot onto pasta.

DESSERTS

I COULD TALK ABOUT DESSERTS UNTIL KINGDOM COME! EVERY SINGLE DISH HERE REMINDS ME OF MY CHILDHOOD IN SOME WAY. THEY SAY THAT 'MAN NEVER GROWS UP', AND IT'S TRUE – I'M STILL A GREAT LOVER OF SWEET THINGS. NOWADAYS, IT'S NOT SO COMMON TO EAT DESSERTS IN AN ITALIAN FAMILY, AS PEOPLE EAT FRESH FRUIT INSTEAD. I WAS LUCKY TO HAVE A MOTHER WHO LOVED SWEET THINGS AS MUCH AS I DO. IN TUSCANY, THE MOST FAMOUS DESSERT IS PANFORTE DI SIENA, A HONEYED CAKE WITH CANDIED PEEL, DRIED FRUIT AND NUTS (SEE PAGE 205). BISCOTTI DI PRATO – ALMOND BISCUITS (SEE PAGE 193) – ARE ALSO POPULAR. IN TUSCAN DESSERTS WE VERY RARELY USE CREAM; WE USE A LITTLE MILK, OLIVE OIL AND BUTTER. DESSERTS ARE EATEN WITH VIN SANTO, A SWEET WINE MADE FROM WHITE GRAPES THAT ARE HARVESTED IN LATE SEPTEMBER OR EARLY OCTOBER, THEN HUNG OR LAID ON STRAW UNTIL CHRISTMAS, SO THE GRAPES BECOME SULTANAS. THE DRIED GRAPES ARE THEN CRUSHED AND ALLOWED TO FERMENT. THEY ARE LEFT IN A SMALL VAT FOR THREE, FIVE, OR TEN YEARS. THE DRINK IS CALLED VIN SANTO OR 'HOLY WINE' BECAUSE IT IS THE WINE DRUNK BY THE PRIEST DURING MASS. WE DIP OUR PUDDINGS IN IT, OR DRINK IT WITH THE PUDDING.

BUDINO DI RISO

RICE PUDDING WITH LEMON

AND CINNAMON

In Tuscany, we tend to associate rice more with sweet dishes than with savoury ones. This recipe is often made as small, oval-shaped cakes. They say that it is the most frequently requested patisserie in the bars in Florence; you eat it with your morning cappuccino. Here, I have given you a recipe for four people – so simply divide it into quarters.

Serves 4

125g/4oz/¾ cup white pudding rice
2 tbsp caster (superfine) sugar, plus extra to serve
about 600ml/1 pint/2½ cups milk
1 tsp ground cinnamon
grated zest of 2 lemons
2 eggs
600ml/1 pint/2½ cups double (heavy) cream

Preheat the oven to 170°C/325°F/Gas Mark 3. Butter an oval glass dish of about 15 × 23cm/6 × 9 inches and at least 5cm/2 inches deep.

Wash the rice and drain well. Put the rice and 1 tbsp of sugar into the dish, with enough of the milk to cover the rice. Stir in the cinnamon and the grated lemon zest, then bake in the oven for half an hour.

While the rice is cooking, stir the remaining sugar and eggs into the cream.

About 10 minutes before the end of cooking, pour the cream and sugar mixture over the rice. When the pudding has become more solid, sprinkle with caster (superfine) sugar and replace in the oven at 180°C/350°F/Gas Mark 4 for 20 minutes.

When brown on top (be careful not to let it burn), remove from the oven and let cool for 1 hour before serving.

PESCHE ALL'AMORETTO

ALVARO'S PEACHES WITH AMARETTI

Serves 4

4 ripe but firm peaches
8 tbsp brown sugar (depending on ripeness
    of fruit)
350ml/12fl oz/1½ cups *vin santo*
8 amaretti biscuits, crushed
8 tbsp runny honey

For the mascarpone cream:
mascarpone cheese
1 tbsp icing (confectioners') sugar
3 tbsp *vin santo*

This recipe came about because one day I had to produce a pudding and all I had in my cupboard was amaretti biscuits and a basket of fresh peaches: this is what I came up with!

Preheat the oven to 180°C/350°F/Gas Mark 4. Halve the peaches, scoop out the stones and enlarge the hole for the filling, if necessary. Sprinkle with brown sugar (if ripe they don't need too much, if hard, be quite liberal) and a little *vin santo*, mixed with water. Put them in an ovenproof dish and bake for 1–2 minutes, depending on how ripe they are.

Remove from the oven and put the crushed amaretti biscuits into the centres of the peaches. Increase the heat of the oven to 200°C/400°F/Gas Mark 6. Pour over a syrup made from runny honey and some more *vin santo*, which has to be quite thick. Each peach must be coated; make sure they all remain upright and tightly packed. Put back in the oven for about 10 minutes; be careful not to let them burn!

To make the mascarpone cream, fold sugar and *vin santo* into the mascarpone.

Serve two peach halves on a plate, pour over the juices and add a spoon of mascarpone cream.

RICCIARELLI DI SIENA

SOFT ALMOND BISCUITS

These biscuits are available around Christmas-time in Italian delicatessens in London and all over the world. In Tuscany, we tend to eat them all year round, although they are officially known as 'Christmas Biscuits'. When I was little, I used to find these on my bedside table in the morning if I had been 'a good boy'! Because they look so white and pure, they are also known as fairy biscuits. This dish needs to stand for 12 hours before cooking.

Makes 30 biscuits

300g/11oz almonds
10g/¼oz bitter almonds (see Note, below)
200g/7oz/1¾ cups icing (confectioners') sugar, plus extra to serve
1 egg white
rice paper

Blanch the almonds in boiling water, then peel them. Toast them in a hot oven, in a dry frying-pan (skillet) or under the grill, then crush them in a mortar with a pestle. Weigh the ground almonds: they should not exceed 200g/7oz in weight.

Mix the sugar with the almonds.

Beat the egg white until stiff and mix with the almonds. Put the mixture in small lumps on to a work surface dusted with icing (confectioners') sugar. Shape the mixture into ovals, then press down on them with the palm of your hand.

Place each oval on a small square of rice paper and arrange on a baking sheet. Let them stand for 12 hours.

Preheat the oven to 120°C/225°F/Gas Mark 1. Put the biscuits into the hot oven and switch off the oven. Leave them overnight, as for meringues. If you don't want to do this, bake them for just over 1 hour at 120°C/225°F/Gas Mark 1, making sure that they do not brown and that they remain soft.

Serve cold, sprinkled with icing (confectioners') sugar.

Note:
Bitter almonds may be available in an Italian delicatessen or greengrocer but, if not, you can break open a peach kernel and use the seeds inside that. Or, to make ordinary sweet almonds bitter, put them in a pan of water with the leaf of an artichoke, heat for 20 minutes till the water is almost boiling. Dry them and they will taste bitter.

FAGOTTI DOLCI DI RICOTTA

RUM AND RICOTTA PARCELS

My grandmother used to make these whenever there was a feast or a birthday in the family, and also at Easter. At Easter time, we used to colour chicken eggs and take them to church with these sweet 'biscuits'. The priest would sprinkle them with holy water, and only then were we allowed to eat them.

Makes 10

350g/12oz bread dough, already risen (use Schiacciata, see page 38, but omit the rosemary)
1 tbsp olive oil, plus extra oil or lard for frying
250g/9oz fresh ricotta cheese, crumbled
100g/4oz/½ cup caster (superfine) sugar
90ml/3fl oz/scant ½ cup rum
vanilla powder
icing (confectioners') sugar, to serve

Incorporate a tablespoon of olive oil into the dough and let it stand for approximately 30 minutes, covered with a clean teatowel.

Mix the ricotta with the sugar in a bowl and then pour in the rum and a pinch of vanilla.

Roll out the dough as thinly as you can (about 2mm thick is ideal) and cut it into 6cm/2½-inch squares. Pile some of the ricotta mixture on half of each square, fold over the other half and seal by pressing the edges together.

Heat the lard or oil in a frying-pan (skillet). When very hot, put the ricotta parcels in and fry until golden on both sides. Drain on kitchen paper and sprinkle with icing (confectioners') sugar.

PAN DI PASQUA

EASTER BUNS

These are very similar to hot-cross buns and are also known as Pane Greco. *This is because we believe that they were introduced to Italy by Paul the Apostle, who brought them from Greece.*

Makes 10 buns

250g/9oz bread dough, already risen (use Schiacciata, see page 38, but omit the rosemary)
4 eggs, beaten
200g/7oz/1 cup caster (superfine) sugar
1 tbsp orange juice
2 tbsp olive oil
pinch of ground cinnamon
1 tbsp aniseeds, ground
plain (all-purpose) white flour for dusting

Knead the bread dough for 5 minutes. Then make a little cross on the surface with a knife, cover with a clean tea towel and let it stand for 1 hour.

Beat the eggs in a basin and blend in the sugar, orange juice, olive oil, cinnamon and aniseeds.

Gradually incorporate the mixture into the bread dough, kneading it gently. When it is well blended, shape into small oval buns. Arrange them on a buttered baking tray dusted with flour.

Make a small cross on each bun, cover with a tea towel and let them stand for 30 minutes.

Preheat the oven to 220°C/425°F/Gas Mark 7. Bake until the buns are golden brown, about 30 minutes.

BISCOTTI DI PRATO

GOLDEN ALMOND BISCUITS

Makes about 50 biscuits

200g/7oz sweet almonds
100g/4oz/1½ cups pine nuts
500g/1lb 2oz/3 cups plain (all-purpose) white
 flour, plus extra for dusting
500g/1lb 2oz/2½ cups caster (superfine) sugar
salt
4 eggs

The best kind of almond biscuits are made in the Tuscan town of Prato. If they come from this town, then they are sold wrapped in blue paper. There can hardly be a family in Italy who does not have a jar of these biscuits in their house – often they will be homemade. They are, for once, correctly called biscuits, since they are literally bis cuit *or 'cooked twice'. They are delicious dipped in* vin santo *and will last for a long time if kept in an airtight container.*

Preheat the oven to 180°C/350°F/Gas Mark 4. Toast the almonds in the oven for a few minutes. Then peel and chop together with the pine nuts.

Pour the flour on to a work surface, mix in the sugar, a pinch of salt and the chopped almonds and pine nuts. Blend in the eggs. Knead until you obtain a soft and elastic dough and then roll out and shape into small loaves.

Butter a baking dish and dust it with flour.

Place the loaves on it and bake them for approximately 25 minutes or until they are a light golden colour.

Remove from the oven, slice to a thickness of 1.5–2cm/⅝–¾ inch and return to the oven to bake until a deep golden brown, about 10 more minutes.

ZUCCOTTO ALLA FIORENTINA

FLORENTINE-STYLE CAKE

Serves 8–10

For the sponge cake:
4 eggs
150g/5oz/½ cup caster (superfine) sugar
grated zest of 1 lemon
salt
75g/3oz/¾ cup plain (all-purpose) white
 flour, sifted
75g/3oz/½ cup potato flour or cornflour,
 sifted

For the topping:
50g/2oz almonds
50g/2oz walnut kernels
50g/2oz hazelnuts
75g/3oz/½ cup chopped dark chocolate
sweet liqueur, e.g. maraschino or rum,
 for soaking
600ml/1 pint/2½ cups double (heavy) cream
100g/4oz/1 cup icing (confectioners') sugar
75g/3oz chocolate buttons or chocolate chips
100g/4oz mixed candied and dried fruit,
 chopped
sweetened cocoa (drinking chocolate)
 to decorate

This is a very well-known Florentine cake: every single patisserie in Florence will have it.

Preheat the oven to 200°C/400°F/Gas Mark 6. Butter and flour a 25cm/10-inch diameter cake tin (pan).

To make the sponge cake: separate the eggs and whisk the yolks with the caster (superfine) sugar, until pale and creamy. Mix in the lemon zest and a pinch of salt. Sift the flours together and whisk them in as well.

Beat the egg whites until stiff and gently fold them into the mixture. Pour into the prepared cake tin and bake for 40 minutes.

Turn out the cake and leave to cool.

To make the topping: blanch the almonds in boiling water; peel them, then toast in the hot oven for a few minutes, with the walnuts and hazelnuts. Peel the nuts by rubbing them in the palms of your hands, and then chop them all together.

Melt the chocolate in the top of a double saucepan or in a heatproof bowl set over a pan of boiling water.

Using a long serrated knife, cut the cake horizontally into slices about 1cm/½ inch thick. Using an upturned bowl about 20–23cm/8–9 inches in diameter, cut out a disc of the cake and set aside. Line the sides of the bowl with strips of the sponge cake. Sprinkle the cake with sweet liqueur to moisten it thoroughly.

Whip the cream and fold in the icing (confectioners') sugar, the chocolate buttons, candied peel and the nuts. Spoon half the cream into the cake-lined bowl, spreading it up the sides.

Fold the melted chocolate into the remaining whipped cream and spoon into the bowl. Cover with the reserved disc of cake, then, cover with foil and refrigerate for a day (the longer, the better). Alternatively, if you are short of time, place in the freezer for a couple of hours.

Remove from the fridge or freezer and turn out upside-down on to a flat plate.

Cut three or four strips of foil, about 1cm/½ inch wide. Place on top of the cake to make a star pattern. Dust the cake with cocoa, then carefully remove the strips of foil.

CRESCENTINE

SWEET FRITTERS

In Tuscany we cook fritters for every occasion. I suppose this is because they are easy for Mamma to make. Some are made for Easter, some for 19 March – the Festival of St Giuseppe – and some (with chestnuts) for All Saints Day on 1 November. There is a lot of baking powder in this recipe but it is quite correct; the crescentine really need to 'balloon' out!

Makes about 20 fritters

300g/11oz/2 cups plain (all-purpose) white flour
100g/4oz baking powder
salt
1 tbsp lard
600ml/1 pint/2½ cups milk
olive oil for deep-frying
caster (superfine) sugar, to serve

Sift the flour, baking powder and a pinch of salt on to a work surface. Work in the lard and enough milk to obtain a soft dough. Cover with a tea towel and let stand for 30 minutes.

Roll out the dough to a thickness of about 5mm/¼ inch, then cut into squares.

Heat the oil for deep-frying until very hot. Fry the fritters, turning them over until golden brown on both sides.

Lift the fritters out of the fat, drain on kitchen paper, dust with sugar and serve hot on a platter.

FRITTELLE DI PASQUA

EASTER FRITTERS

At Easter time during my childhood we did not have a tradition of eating chocolate. We had to use the ingredients that were available to us, and fritters were a very easy thing to make. This recipe is almost like fried pasta.

Makes 10–15

4 eggs
caster (superfine) sugar to taste, plus extra to serve
200g/7oz/1½ cups plain (all-purpose) white flour
salt
grated zest of 1 lemon
50g/2oz raisins, soaked in water
lard for deep-frying

Separate the eggs and beat the yolks with the sugar until well mixed. Stir in the flour, a pinch of salt and the lemon zest.

Whisk the egg whites until stiff and fold into the mixture. Drain and squeeze the raisins dry and add them to the mixture.

Heat the lard for deep-frying. Scoop up spoonfuls of batter and drop into the hot lard, frying them until golden brown on both sides.

Lift the fritters out of the fat, drain on kitchen paper, dust with sugar and serve on a platter.

TORTA DOLCE DI BIETOLE

SWEET SWISS CHARD PIE

This is a very famous pie which my grandmother made often when swiss chard was in season. We would make cakes out of any ingredients that were available, so although this sounds rather unusual, it was a fairly common dish for me.

Serves 10

For the dough:
300g/11oz/2 cups plain (all-purpose) white flour
125g/4½oz/1 cup butter
75g/3oz/⅓ cup caster (superfine) sugar
salt
2 eggs, separated

For the filling:
500g/1lb 2oz swiss chard
30g/1oz/2 tbsp butter
75g/3oz/⅓ cup caster (superfine) sugar
50g/2oz/1 cup pine nuts
30g/1oz raisins, soaked in warm water and squeezed
grated nutmeg and ground cinnamon

To make the dough
Put the flour on a work surface, make a hole in the middle with your fist and work in the butter, sugar, a pinch of salt and the egg yolks. Knead the ingredients together until you have a soft and smooth dough. Cover with a teatowel and let stand in a warm place for 2 hours. Reserve the egg whites.

To make the filling
Clean the swiss chard, discarding the hard parts, wash and cook briefly in the water clinging to the leaves. Squeeze dry, chop and sauté in the butter for a few minutes. Put it in a bowl and mix with the sugar, pine nuts, raisins and a pinch each of nutmeg and cinnamon.

Preheat the oven to 190°C/375°F/Gas Mark 5.
   Roll out the dough and line a buttered and floured ovenproof dish with half of the dough. Pour in the chard mixture and cover with the rest of the dough, sealing it well around the edges. Brush with the beaten egg whites and bake for 25–30 minutes.

TORTA DI RISO

VANILLA RICE CAKE

This cake was a favourite of my Auntie Dailia, who used to bake it for me even when she was well over eighty years old.

Serves 6–10

900ml/1½ pints/3¾ cups milk
250g/9oz/1¼ cups white rice
flour for dusting
3 eggs, beaten
150g/5oz/⅔ cup caster (superfine) sugar
50g/2oz mixed pine nuts and walnut kernels, roughly chopped
100g/4oz candied orange and lime peel
pinch of vanilla powder
grated zest of 1 lemon
30g/1oz/2 tbsp butter

To decorate:
sweetened cocoa (drinking chocolate)
icing (confectioners') sugar

Pour the milk into a saucepan and bring to the boil. Add the rice and cook for about 20 minutes. When the rice is well cooked, remove from the heat and leave to cool.

Preheat the oven to 190°C/375°F/Gas Mark 5. Butter a 25cm/10-inch cake tin (pan) and sprinkle with flour. Tip out any excess flour.

Mix the eggs, sugar, pine nuts, walnuts, candied peel, vanilla, the lemon zest and butter. Blend this mixture with the cooled rice, then pour into the cake tin (pan). Bake for 25 minutes.

Remove the cake from the tin (pan) and sprinkle with cocoa mixed with icing (confectioners') sugar.

CASTAGNACCIO

CHESTNUT CAKE

This is a very well known cake in Tuscany, especially in the area of Lucca. There are several variations to this recipe: you can add walnuts and orange peel or more or less olive oil. Some people prefer the castagnaccio *very thin and crunchy; others thicker, 2cm/⅜ inch deep. Or you can mix the flour only with water, pour into the baking dish, then add the rosemary, raisins, pine nuts and walnuts on top of the batter.*

Serves 10–20

300g/11oz chestnut flour
1 tbsp pine nuts
150g/5oz raisins
salt

For the topping:
fresh rosemary leaves
olive oil

Preheat the oven to 180°C/350°F/Gas Mark 4. In a bowl, mix the chestnut flour, pine nuts, raisins and a pinch of salt. Add enough water to make a rather liquid batter and stir well to eliminate any lumps.

Grease a shallow ovenproof dish. Pour in the mixture to a thickness of about 1 cm/½ inch. Sprinkle with rosemary leaves and a little olive oil.

Bake for about 30 minutes or until the top has become crisp.

SCHIACCIATA CON L'UVA

GRAPE BREAD

Serves 10–12

350g/12oz bread dough, already risen (use
Schiacciata, see page 38, but omit the
rosemary)
2 tbsp lard
1 tbsp caster (superfine) sugar
1 bunch of black grapes
1 tbsp icing (confectioners') sugar

*My mother made this delicious bread whenever we had grapes –
from September until the end of November. She used to keep the
grapes hanging from the ceiling in the kitchen until they became
like sultanas. Up to that time, she would bake this bread about
once a week every time she made her other bread.*

Work the dough on a work surface, blending in a heaped
tablespoon of lard and the sugar. Cover with a clean tea towel and
let stand for an hour.

Put the dough back on the work surface and knead it again for
a few minutes. Roll it out fairly thickly with a rolling pin, then
divide it in half.

Grease a baking dish with the remaining lard and line it with
one half of the dough. Cover the entire surface with grapes, place
the rest of the dough on top and garnish with a few more grapes.
Cover the baking dish with a cloth and let stand for another hour.

Preheat the oven to 180°C/350°F/Gas Mark 4. Bake the bread
for 30 minutes.

FRITTELLE DI CASTAGNE

CHESTNUT-FLOUR FRITTERS

This is another recipe that used to entice my uncle into coming to stay unexpectedly. His nickname was 'Zio Moro' – we called him this because he was the only one on my father's side of the family to have dark hair. These fritters are usually made for All Saints Day on 1 November.

Makes about 20

300g/11oz/2 cups chestnut flour
1 tbsp raisins
2 tbsp pine nuts
leaves of 1 fresh rosemary sprig
salt
olive oil for deep-frying
caster (superfine) sugar, to serve

Mix the flour with the raisins, pine nuts, rosemary leaves, a pinch of salt and enough water to make a thick mixture.

Heat the oil for deep-frying-until very hot. Scoop spoonfuls of the mixture into the oil and fry until golden brown.

Drain on kitchen paper and serve hot, sprinkled with sugar.

LATTE COTTO

SPICED MILK PUDDING

This is a fairly light dish that was given to me by a lady who ran one of the greatest patisseries in Pistoia. Her name was Signora Carabbi, and whenever I used to pass by the shop, if she had some freshly made milk pudding she would bang on her window and call me in.

Serves 8–10

4 eggs
75g/3oz/¾ cup plain (all-purpose) white flour
1 tbsp sugar
pinch each of ground cinnamon, vanilla powder and grated nutmeg
1 litre/1¾ pints/4½ cups very creamy milk
butter
1 lemon, peeled

Preheat the oven to 220°C/425°F/Gas Mark 7.

Beat the eggs in a bowl, blend in the flour, sugar and spices and stir, gradually pouring in the milk. Add a little butter if the milk isn't very creamy. Add the lemon peel and leave to infuse for a few minutes.

Butter a shallow ovenproof dish and dust it with flour. Pour in the batter in and bake for approximately 30 minutes.

Serve cold, cut into pieces.

FRITTELLE DI MELE

APPLE FRITTERS

A very kind friend of mine named Walter gave me this recipe. He is from northern Italy and is a resident chef at a cookery school there. In Tuscany, people often make these fritters for the Feast of the Madonna.

Makes 20

2 eggs
3 tbsp plain (all-purpose) white flour
1 tbsp olive oil
salt
4 apples
olive oil for deep-frying
icing (confectioners') sugar, to serve

Beat together the eggs, flour and oil, with a pinch of salt. Add as much water as is necessary to make a soft, but not too runny, mixture.

Peel and core the apples, being careful not to break them, and cut into thin discs. Dip the apple discs into the batter to coat thoroughly.

Heat the oil for deep-frying until very hot, then fry the apple discs until golden on both sides. Drain on kitchen paper, dust with sugar and serve.

FRITTELLE DI RISO

RAISIN AND RICE FRITTERS

Whenever Mamma made these, my uncle used to arrive on our doorstep – I don't know how, as we had no telephone in those days. It's still a mystery to me how he knew! They are very often made for Christmas.

Makes 20–25

200g/7oz/1 cup pudding or Italian arborio rice
500ml/17fl oz/2¼ cups milk
1 tbsp plain (all-purpose) white flour
2 eggs, beaten
grated zest of 1 lemon
50g/2oz raisins, soaked in water, drained and squeezed dry
1 tbsp sugar
salt
oil and lard for deep-frying
caster (superfine) sugar, to serve

Cook the rice in the milk until very well done.

Add the flour, eggs, lemon zest, raisins, sugar and a pinch of salt. Stir well.

Heat the oil and lard for deep-frying. Scoop up spoonfuls of the mixture and drop into the hot oil. Fry until golden brown. Lift them out of the oil and drain on kitchen paper. Dust with sugar and serve.

PANFORTE DI SIENA

HONEYED PEEL AND NUT CAKE

This is the most famous Tuscan dessert you can think of – the Tuscan Christmas Pudding. The recipe for Panforte is one of the most closely guarded secrets of Siena, and it's an unwritten law that it should remain as such. However, I have dared to give it to you because originally I come from that part of the world, so I have the right to disclose it! My mother would use her own dried figs and honey from our beehives to make this.

Serves 6

200g/7oz almonds
100g/4oz walnut kernels
100g/4oz hazelnuts
300g/11oz candied pumpkin, lemon and orange peel, very finely chopped
100g/4oz/¾ cup dried figs, chopped
50g/2oz/½ cup sweetened cocoa (drinking chocolate)
2 tbsp mixed ground cinnamon, cloves, coriander, white pepper and nutmeg
100g/4oz honey
150g/5oz/1¼ cups icing (confectioners') sugar
1 heaped tbsp plain (all-purpose) white flour, plus a little extra
rice paper

Preheat the oven to 160°C/325°F/Gas Mark 3. Blanch the almonds, walnuts and hazelnuts in boiling water for 3 minutes.

Peel the nuts, then toast them for a few minutes in a hot oven, under a hot grill or in a dry frying-pan (skillet); then grind them.

In a bowl, mix the ground nuts with the candied peel, figs, cocoa and spices. Stir with a wooden spoon until well mixed.

Put the honey in a heatproof basin, then place in a saucepan of boiling water. Warm the honey and stir in the sugar. The honey has reached the right consistency when it forms a thread if you touch the surface with your finger and lift it upwards.

Remove the basin from the heat, stir in the flour and the fruit and nut mixture, then pour into a buttered ovenproof dish lined with rice paper. Sprinkle a little more flour over the top. Bake for approximately 40 minutes.

CAVALLUCCI SENESI

BISCUITS FROM SIENA

These biscuits remind me of when I was young. On my way back from school I used to have one lire to spend on sweets. These cavallucci were the cheapest and most delicious thing you could buy, so I used to spend my pocket money on them. They are usually made only in winter, for Christmas or for carnival in January and February.

Makes 10–15 biscuits

100g/4oz honey
250g/9oz/1¼ cups caster (superfine) sugar
350g/12oz/2½ cups plain (all-purpose) white flour
50g/2oz walnut kernels
50g/2oz candied lemon and orange peel, chopped
pinch of aniseeds, ground in a mortar
pinch of ground cinnamon
pinch of ground coriander
pinch of grated nutmeg

Preheat the oven to 130°C/250°F/Gas Mark 2. Heat the honey in a heatproof bowl placed over a pan of boiling water. Stir in the sugar and cook until it forms a thread when you take a little bit of mixture between your finger and thumb; first dip your fingers in water.

Remove the bowl from the heat and gently stir in the flour with a wooden spoon, pouring it in gradually. Add the walnuts, the peel, the aniseeds and the spices.

Roll out the dough quite thickly, about 2.5cm/1 inch thick, on a floured work surface. Cut into small squares or ovals and place on a buttered baking sheet, dusted with flour.

Bake for 5 minutes and then turn off the oven and leave them overnight to cook in the cooling oven. If you don't want to do this, bake them for just under 1 hour. They should be yellow and quite brittle.

TORTA DI MANDORLE

ALMOND CAKE

This cake was the reason that I was attracted to the window of the patisserie as a child, yet when I eventually tasted it, I didn't like it! Now I realize that it's a fantastically delicious thing. Even today, you will see it in the window of almost every patisserie in Italy, its surface glinting with a shiny sugary glaze.

Serves 10

60g/2oz almonds
15g/½oz bitter almonds (see Note, page 190)
175g/6oz/1¼ cups plain (all-purpose) white flour
300g/11oz/1½ cups caster (superfine) sugar
9 eggs
grated zest of 1 lemon
2 tbsp icing (confectioners') sugar

Preheat the oven to 160°C/325°F/Gas Mark 3. Toast the almonds in a hot oven, under the grill or in a dry frying-pan (skillet). Peel them, then grind them with a pestle and mortar or – carefully, as they must not be powdery – in a food processor.

In a bowl, blend the flour, 1 tbsp of caster (superfine) sugar and the ground almonds.

Separate the eggs, beat the yolks with the remaining caster (superfine) sugar until pale, thick and creamy, then stir these into the almond mixture, with the lemon zest.

Whisk the egg whites until stiff and fold these in as well, gently mixing all the ingredients together until well blended.

Butter and flour an ovenproof dish, pour in the mixture and bake for 30–35 minutes or until the surface is golden brown.

Dust with icing (confectioners') sugar and serve on a platter.

For a special occasion you can decorate the cake by sprinkling with whole or flaked almonds before baking. Before serving, brush with a simple apricot glaze.

CENCI

PASTA RIBBON BISCUITS

These biscuits are made at any time and on any weekend throughout Italy. Their shape and size may change, depending on the region. You could call this a sweet pasta dish.

Makes about 20 biscuits

250g/9oz/1 cup plain (all-purpose) white flour
75g/3oz/$\frac{1}{3}$ cup caster (superfine) sugar, plus extra to serve
2 tbsp olive oil
grated zest of 1 orange or 1 lemon
2 tbsp *vin santo* (or dessert wine)
2 eggs, beaten
salt
olive oil for frying

Put the flour on a work surface, make a hole in the middle with your fist and work in the sugar, the olive oil, orange or lemon zest, the *vin santo* or wine, the eggs and a pinch of salt. Knead until you have a soft dough; then let stand for 30 minutes.

Roll the dough out quite thinly and cut into rectangles and squares with a pastry cutter.

Heat the oil to a fairly high temperature in a frying-pan (skillet) and fry the shapes until golden on both sides. Drain on kitchen paper and serve on a platter, dusted with sugar.

CALDARROSTE UBRIACHE

TIPSY CHESTNUTS

You will find these being sold on many a street in Tuscany; they are also served after dinner, sprinkled with grappa while still hot. Watch out, as the hot grappa can make you cough when you take your first mouthful!

Serves 10

1kg/2lb chestnuts
100g/4oz/1 cup caster (superfine) sugar
90ml/3fl oz/scant $\frac{1}{2}$ cup grappa

Cut into the hull of each chestnut, then put the chestnuts in a old frying-pan (skillet) in the bottom of which you have drilled holes. Alternatively, use an old metal colander. Grill the chestnuts over hot embers or a gas flame, sprinkling them with water a couple of times.

When they are ready, the husk will start to come apart and the skin inside will come off easily. Skin, place in a heavy-based saucepan, cover with sugar and sprinkle with the grappa.

Light the grappa and serve the chestnuts very hot.

PAN DEI SANTI

BREAD OF THE SAINTS

This is made at the beginning of November for All Saints Day. It is also known as 'the Bread of the Dead'. We actually used to take this bread to the graveyards to offer to our dead for their own feast.

Serves 10

50g/2oz walnut kernels
50g/2oz sweet almonds
300g/11oz bread dough, risen (use Schiacciata, see page 38, but omit the rosemary)
1 tbsp olive oil
30g/1oz raisins
aniseeds, ground
grated lemon zest

Blanch the walnuts and the almonds in boiling water. Peel them, then toast them for a few minutes in a hot oven, under the grill or in a dry frying-pan (skillet); then chop them.

Knead the oil into the bread dough with the nuts, raisins, aniseeds and lemon zest. Cover with a tea towel and let stand in a warm place for 30 minutes.

Preheat the oven to 180°C/350°F/Gas Mark 4. Butter and flour a baking sheet. Cut a cross on the dough, place it on the sheet and bake for about 40 minutes.

BUCCELLATO

SWEET BREAKFAST BREAD

This type of bread looks like hot-cross buns. It is made all year round in the area around Lucca. Sliced, it is served for breakfast, with coffee, instead of croissants. Indeed, croissants and brioche are French introductions but buccellato *was eaten in Italy before Catherine de Medici had even been to France.*

Serves 10

400g/14oz/3½ cups plain (all-purpose) white flour
150g/5oz/⅔ cup caster (superfine) sugar
pinch of salt
pinch of bicarbonate of soda (baking soda)
2 eggs
50g/2oz/¼ cup butter, softened
grated zest of 1 lemon
10g/¼oz fresh yeast or 15g sachet of active dried yeast
2 tbsp warm milk

Put the flour on a work surface and mix with the sugar, salt and bicarbonate of soda. Make a hole in the middle with your fist and blend in the eggs, butter, lemon zest and the yeast, dissolved in the warm milk. Knead until well blended, cover with a tea towel and leave for 2 hours.

Heat the oven to 180°C/350°F/Gas Mark 4. Turn the dough out on to a floured work surface and knead again, then roll it out. Butter a rectangular loaf tin (pan) or a ring mould (tube pan) and dust it with flour.

Place the rolled out dough in the tin (pan) and bake for 35–40 minutes until golden.

BRUTTI E BUONI

TOASTED ALMOND BISCUITS

*These biscuits are a speciality from Montecatini. Their name describes them perfectly, as they are ugly (*brutti*) but they taste very good (*buoni*)! They are not supposed to be carefully rolled or cut out, but dropped on the baking sheet just as they are.*

Makes 20 biscuits

300g/11oz almonds
20g/³⁄₄oz bitter almonds (see Note, page 190)
4 egg whites
250g/9oz/1¹⁄₄ cups caster (superfine) sugar

Blanch the almonds in boiling water, peel them, then toast in the oven, under the grill or in a dry frying-pan (skillet) for a few minutes; then chop them.

Whisk the egg whites until stiff. Fold in the almonds and sugar. Pour the mixture into a saucepan and cook over a very low heat for 20 minutes.

Heat the oven to 180°C/350°F/Gas Mark 4. Butter and flour a baking sheet. Scoop spoonfuls of the cooked mixture onto the baking sheet. Bake for about 45 minutes or until golden brown.

These biscuits keep well in a sealed biscuit tin.

BOMBOLINI ALLA FIORENTINA

FLORENTINE DOUGHNUTS

This recipe dates back to the 1200s. I suppose they were the first doughnuts ever made in the world. In more recent times, you could often find them being sold outside cinemas from small trolleys – just like Trippa alla Fiorentina (see page 118).

Makes about 10 doughnuts

500g/1lb 2oz/4½ cups plain (all-purpose) white flour
75g/3oz/⅓ cup caster (superfine) sugar, plus extra to serve
grated zest of 1 lemon
salt
75g/3oz/¾ cup butter, softened
10g/¼ oz fresh yeast or 15g sachet of active dried yeast
90ml/3fl oz/scant ½ cup warm milk
olive oil for deep-frying

Pile the flour on a work surface and mix it with the sugar, lemon zest and a pinch of salt. Blend in the butter and the yeast, dissolved in the warm milk. Knead the dough until soft and pliable, adding a little more warm milk, if necessary. Cover with a tea towel and let stand for a couple of hours.

Knead again and roll out to a thickness of about 1cm/½ inch. Cut into round shapes, using either a pastry cutter or an upturned glass, and place these on a floured work surface to rest for a further hour.

Heat the oil for deep-frying and fry the discs until golden on both sides. Drain on kitchen paper and sprinkle with sugar.

TIRAMISU

PICK-ME UP!

In every part of Italy, every town or village, the people will tell you that this originally comes from their part of the world. We do not know the true origin of it but the recipe started when the yolk of an egg was whipped with sugar. Sponge fingers were dipped in the eggy mixture and Mamma would make it for every child before he went to school. Tiramisu literally means 'pick-me-up' and implies that the child would grow up strong and healthy. As we grew up, Marsala and other wines were added to the recipe and this eventually became the dessert we all know so well.

Serves 10

strong black coffee for dipping
175ml/6fl oz/¾ cup *vin santo*
20 savoiardi biscuits (sponge fingers or ladyfingers)
5 eggs, separated
350g/12oz/1⅓ cups caster (superfine) sugar
500g/1lb 2oz mascarpone cheese
rum or brandy (optional)
grated chocolate or sweetened cocoa (drinking chocolate)

Mix the coffee and *vin santo* together. Dip about half the biscuits briefly in this mixture, so they are soaked but not soggy, and line a 23cm/9-inch cake tin (pan) with half the biscuits. Sprinkle the remaining coffee mixture over any that look too dry.

Whisk the egg yolks and sugar together until light and creamy. Add the mascarpone and then beat until fairly thick.

Whisk the egg whites until thick but not stiff and fold them into the egg yolk mixture. Add a little rum or brandy to this mixture, if desired.

Put half this mixture into the lined cake tin (pan) and then put a layer of soaked biscuits on top. Then cover with the remaining mixture. Leave overnight in the fridge.

Turn out on to a plate and serve sprinkled with grated chocolate or cocoa.

INDEX

Page numbers in *italic* refer to the illustrations

agnello al forno, 131
agnello in salsa, 132, *133*
agnello montealbano, 134
almonds: almond cake, *208*, 209
   golden almond biscuits, 193, *193*
   soft almond biscuits, 190, *191*
   toasted almond biscuits, 214, *215*
Alvaro's peaches with amaretti, 189, *189*
anatra all'Aretina, 96
anchovy cake, 157
anguilla marinata, 152, *153*
apple fritters, 202
aqua cotta, 18
Aretina chicken, 92, *93*
Aretina duck, 96
arista alla Fiorentina, 128, *129*
arrosto di cinghiale, 130
arrosto di vitello, 126, *127*
artichokes: artichoke sauce, 176
   baked artichoke cake, *26*, 27
   farmhouse artichokes, 58
   Florentine-style artichokes, 53
   fried baby artichokes, *54*, 55
   mixed meat and vegetable fritters, 119
   risotto with baby artichokes, 172, *173*
asparagus, penne with prosciutto and, 77, *77*

baccala alla Fiorentina, 151
baccala bianco, 150
baccala e ceci, 150
baccelli stufati, 56, *57*
bacon: rice and olive salad, 171
   see also pancetta
baker's pasta, 70
basil: baker's pasta, 70
   risotto with basil sauce, 170
   summer sauce, 182, *183*
beans *see* cannellini beans; french beans
beef: beefsteak casserole, 109
   Florentine beef stew, 106
   Florentine braised beef, 108
   Florentine steak, 112
   half-cooked slices of beef, 106, *107*
   peasant beef meatloaf, 113
   Pistoiese meat sauce, 178, *179*

sliced fillet of beef with corn salad, *110*, 111
soup of minced (ground) beef, pancetta and vegetables, 11
bianchetti alla Versigliese, 156
biscotti di Prato, 193, *193*
biscuits: biscuits from Siena, 206, *207*
   golden almond biscuits, 193, *193*
   pasta ribbon biscuits, 210
   soft almond biscuits, 190, *191*
   toasted almond biscuits, 214, *215*
bistecca alla Fiorentina, 112
bomboloni alla Fiorentina, 216, *217*
bread: baked quails in bread parcels, 94
   bread and tomato soup, 10
   bread of the saints, 211
   buccellato, 212, *213*
   Easter buns, 192
   focaccia, 24, *25*
   grape bread, 200, *200*
   oven-baked goose, 95
   rum and ricotta parcels, 192
   sage and rosemary bread, 38
   tomato and bread salad, 38, *39*
broad (fava) beans, stewed, 56, *57*
broccoli sauce, 182
brutti e buoni, 214, *215*
buccellato, 212, *213*
budino di riso, 188

cabbage, polenta with beans and, *30*, 31
cacciucco, 163
cakes: almond cake, *208*, 209
   chestnut cake, 198, *199*
   Florentine-style cake, *194*, 195
   honeyed peel and nut cake, *204*, 205
   vanilla rice cake, 198
calamari con bietole, 144, *145*
caldarroste ubriache, 210
calves' kidneys *see* kidneys
calves' liver *see* liver
cannellini beans: farmhouse soup, 19
   flask-cooked beans, 50, *51*
   Florentine beans, *46*, 47
   polenta with cabbage and, *30*, 31
   rice and olive salad, 171
   risotto with, 169
   thick bean soup, 20, *21*
   Tuscan bean stew, 47
carciofi alla paesana, 58
carciofi in piede alla Fiorentina, 53
carciofini fritti, *54*, 55
castagnaccio, 198, *199*

cavallucci Senesi, 206, *207*
celery, farmhouse, 59
cenci, 210
cheese: baked vegetable lasagne, 80, *81*
   baker's pasta, 70
   naked gnocchi, 74
   pasta twists with sun-dried tomatoes, 63, *63*
   penne with asparagus and prosciutto, 77, *77*
   potato dumplings, 76
   rum and ricotta parcels, 192
   stuffed chicken, 90
chestnuts: chestnut cake, 198, *199*
   chestnut-flour fritters, 201
   risotto with chestnuts, 167
   tipsy chestnuts, 210
chicken: Aretina chicken, 92, *93*
   chicken Barontana, 85, *85*
   chicken soup, 18
   Florentine chicken, 88, *89*
   fried chicken, 86
   kebabs of wild boar sausages with chicken, 116, *117*
   stuffed chicken, 90
   with devilled sauce, 86, *87*
   with lemon sauce, 84
   with wild fennel seeds, 91
chicken livers *see* liver
chickpeas: chickpea cake, 35
   pasta and chickpea soup, 20
   salt cod with chickpeas, 150
chocolate: Florentine-style cake, *194*, 195
   sweet and sour hare, 101
le ciacce fritte, 27
cime di rape saltate, 48
cipolle alla grossetana, 44
clam soup, 140
coniglio alla cacciatora, 100
coniglio in tegame, 100
cooked water soup, 18
corn salad, sliced fillet of beef with, *110*, 111
country-style tomato sauce, 181
courgettes (zucchini): mixed meat and vegetable fritters, 119
crescentine, 196
crostini con fegatini di pollo, 28, *29*
cucumber: soup of the Moors, 16, *17*
cuttlefish with peas, 146, *147*

devilled sauce, chicken with, 86, *87*
doughnuts, Florentine, 216, *217*
'drunken' tuna fish, 160, *161*

duck: Aretina duck, 96
  pasta ribbons with duck sauce, 69
dumplings: potato dumplings, 76
  rice dumplings with meat sauce, 168, *168*

Easter buns, 192
Easter fritters, 196
eel, marinated, 152, *153*
eggs *see* omelettes

fagiano al cartoccio, 97
fagiano al tartufo nero, 99
fagiano alla pancetta, 98
fagioli al fiasco, 50, *51*
fagioli alla Fiorentina, 46, *47*
fagioli all'uccelletto, 47
fagiolini alla Fiorentina, 45, *45*
fagotti dolci di ricotta, 192
farmhouse artichokes, 58
farmhouse celery, 59
farmhouse omelette, *34, 35*
farmhouse risotto, 171
farmhouse soup, 19
fava beans *see* broad beans
fegatini con funghi trifolati, 102, *103*
fegato alla Fiorentina, 118
fennel seeds: chicken with wild fennel seeds, 91
fettine di manzo semi cotte, 106, *107*
fettuccine all'anatra, 69
fiori di zucca fritti, 56
fish and seafood, 136–63
  deep-fried mixed fish, 162
  fish soup, 148, *149*
  traditional Tuscan fish stew, 163
  see also mussels, salt cod, tuna etc
flask-cooked beans, 50, *51*
Florentine beans, *46, 47*
Florentine beef stew, 106
Florentine braised beef, 108
Florentine calves' liver, 118
Florentine chicken, 88, *89*
Florentine doughnuts, 216, *217*
Florentine french beans, 45, *45*
Florentine meatballs, 135
Florentine roast loin of pork, 128, *129*
Florentine salt cod, 151
Florentine steak, 112
Florentine-style artichokes, 53
Florentine-style cake, *194,* 195
Florentine tripe, 118
focaccia, 24, *25*
french beans, Florentine, 45, *45*

frittata alla contadina, 34, 35
frittata con pancetta, 32
frittata di bietole, 32, *33*
frittelle di castagne, 201
frittelle di mele, 202
frittelle di Pasqua, 196
frittelle di riso, 202, *203*
fritters: apple, 202
  chestnut-flour, 201
  deep-fried marrow flowers, 56
  Easter, 196
  fried baby artichokes, *54, 55*
  mixed meat and vegetable, 119
  mixed vegetable, 36, *37*
  raisin and rice, 202, *203*
  sweet, 196
fritto misto di carni, 119
funghi alla Toscana, 52
fusilli con pomodori secchi, 63, *63*

garlic sauce, octopus with, 141
garmugia, 11
globe artichokes *see* artichokes
gnocchi: naked gnocchi, 74
  oven-baked gnocchi, *72,* 73
  polenta gnocchi, 74, *75*
gnocchi di farina gialla, 74, *75*
gnocchi di spinaci al forno, 72, 73
gnudi, 74
goose, oven-baked, 95
grape bread, 200, *200*
grappa: tipsy chestnuts, 210

ham *see* prosciutto
hare: pasta with hare sauce, 66, *67*
  sweet and sour hare, 101
honeyed peel and nut cake, *204,* 205
hunter's rabbit, 100

insalata di riso con olive, 171
involtini di vitello, 122
Italian sausages with turnip tops or spinach,
  114, *115*
kebabs of wild boar sausages with chicken,
  116, *117*
kidneys: calves' kidneys with balsamic vinegar,
  120, *121*

lamb: lamb casserole with parsley, 132, *133*
  mixed meat and vegetable fritters, 119
  oven-baked lamb, 131
  pasta ribbons with mutton sauce, 68

  roast leg of lamb with black olives, 134
lasagne, baked vegetable, 80, *81*
lasagne di magro, 80, *81*
latte cotto, 201
lemon: baked mackerel with lemon juice, 160
  chicken with lemon sauce, 84
  rice pudding with lemon and cinnamon,
  188
lepre all'agrodolce, 101
liver: chicken liver sauce, 177
  chicken-liver toasts, 28, *29*
  chicken livers with porcini, 102, *103*
  farmhouse celery, 59
  Florentine calves' liver, 118
Livornese oysters, 141
Livornese red mullet, 154, *155*
Livornese whitebait, 156

mackerel, baked with lemon juice, 160
Maremma-style red mullet, 156
marinated eel, 152, *153*
marrow flowers, deep-fried, 56
meatloaf, peasant beef, 113
milk pudding, spiced, 201
miller's soup, 15
miller's trout, 162
minestra di farro, 15
muscoli ripieni alla Pistoiese, 142, *143*
mushrooms: chicken livers with porcini, 102,
  103
  mushroom casserole, 52
  peasant-style pasta, 70, *71*
mussels: mussel soup, 138, *139*
  stuffed mussels, *142,* 143

naked gnocchi, 74
nodino di vitello al pomodoro, 124, *125*
noodles with ham sauce, 78, *79*

oca al forno, 95
octopus with garlic sauce, 141
olives: baked mackerel with lemon juice, 160
  chicken Barontana, 85, *85*
  rice and olive salad, 171
  roast leg of lamb with black olives, 134
omelettes: bacon, 32
  farmhouse, *34,* 35
  swiss chard, 32, *33*
onions: beefsteak casserole, 109
  Tuscan stuffed onions, 44
ostriche alla Livornese, 141
oven-baked gnocchi, *72,* 73

oven-baked goose, 95
oven-baked lamb, 131
oysters, Livornese, 141

pan dei santi, 211
pan di Pasqua, 192
pancetta: bacon omelette, 32
　　chicken with wild fennel seeds, 91
　　Florentine braised beef, 108
　　Florentine-style artichokes, 53
　　pheasant with black truffles, 99
　　pheasant with pancetta, 98
　　risotto with cannellini beans, 169
　　roast pheasant in paper parcels, 97
　　stewed broad (fava) beans, 56, *57*
panforte di Siena, 204, 205
panzanella, 38, *39*
pappa al pomodoro, 10
pappardelle: pasta with hare sauce, 66, *67*
pappardelle al sugo di pecora, 68
pappardelle con la lepre, 66, *67*
Parma ham *see* prosciutto
pasta, 60–81
　　baked vegetable lasagne, 80, *81*
　　baker's pasta, 70
　　making pasta, 62
　　noodles with ham sauce, 78, *79*
　　pasta and chickpea soup, 20
　　pasta ribbons with duck sauce, 69
　　pasta ribbons with lamb sauce, 68
　　pasta twists with sun-dried tomatoes, 63, *63*
　　pasta with hare sauce, 66, *67*
　　peasant-style pasta, 70, *71*
　　potato dumplings, 76
　　summer pasta salad, 64, *65*
pasta alla contadina, 70, 71
pasta d'estate, 64, 65
pasta e ceci, 20
pasta e fagioli, 20, 21
pasta ribbon biscuits, 210
pastasciutta alla fornaia, 70
peaches with amaretti, 189, *189*
peas: Aretina chicken, 92, *93*
　　cuttlefish with peas, 146, *147*
　　pea casserole, 48, *49*
　　pea sauce, 184
peasant beef meatloaf, 113
peasant-style pasta, 70, *71*
penne con prosciutto e asparagi, 77, 77
peperonata, 40, *41*
peppers: grilled pepper salad, 40, *41*
pesce spada in umido, 158, 159

pesche all'amaretti, 189, *189*
pesciolini fritti, 162
pheasant: roast pheasant in paper parcels, 97
　　with black truffles, 99
　　with pancetta, 98
Pistoiese meat sauce, 178, *179*
pizzas: fried pizzas, 27
　　small thin pizzas, 24, *25*
polenta: polenta gnocchi, 74, *75*
　　with beans and cabbage, *30*, 31
polenta di fagioli e cavolo, 30, 31
pollo ai semi di finocchio, 91
pollo alla diavola, 86, 87
pollo al limone, 84
pollo alla Barontana, 85, 85
pollo alla Fiorentina, 88, *89*
pollo all'Aretina, 92, *93*
pollo farcito, 90
pollo fritto, 86
polpette alla Fiorentina, 135
polpettine di riso al sugo, 168, 168
polpettone alla contadina, 113
polipi in padella, 141
porcini, chicken livers with, 102, *103*
pork: Florentine beans, *46*, 47
　　Florentine roast loin of pork, 128, *129*
potatoes: Florentine meatballs, 135
　　potato dumplings, 76
　　potato soup, 10
prosciutto: Aretina duck, 96
　　grilled pepper (bell pepper) salad, 40, *41*
　　Maremma-style red mullet, 156
　　noodles with ham sauce, 78, *79*
　　penne with asparagus and, 77, *77*
　　pheasant with black truffles, 99
　　risotto with baby artichokes, 172, *173*
pumpkin soup, 14

quaglie in fagotto, 94
quails, baked in bread parcels, 94

rabbit: hunter's rabbit, 100
　　in tomato and wine sauce, 100
ragu di carne alla Pistoiese, 178, 179
raisins: chestnut cake, 198, *199*
　　raisin and rice fritters, 202, *203*
red mullet: Livornese red mullet, 154, *155*
　　Maremma-style red mullet, 156
ribolitta, 10, *13*
ricciarelli di Siena, 190, *191*
rice: Aretina chicken, 92, *93*
　　raisin and rice fritters, 202, *203*

rice and olive salad, 171
rice dumplings with meat sauce, 168, *168*
rice pudding with lemon and cinnamon, 188
vanilla rice cake, 198
riso e castagne, 167
risotto, 164–73
　　farmhouse risotto, 171
　　with baby artichokes, 172, *173*
　　with basil sauce, 170
　　with cannellini beans, 169
　　with chestnuts, 167
　　with sausage sauce, 167
risotto al basilico, 170
risotto alla contadina, 171
risotto con carciofi, 172, 173
risotto con fagioli, 169
risotto con le salsicce, 167
rognoncini all'aceto balsamico, 120, 121
rosemary: Florentine chicken, 88, *89*
　　sage and rosemary bread, 38
rum and ricotta parcels, 192

salads: grilled pepper (bell pepper), 40, *41*
　　rice and olive, 171
　　summer pasta, 64, *65*
　　tomato and bread, 38, *39*
salsa al dragoncello, 180
salsa bianca, 176
salsa cruda, 182, 183
salsa di broccoli, 182
salsa di carciofi per la pasta, 176
salsa di piselli, 184
salsa di pomodoro, 185
salsa fegatini di pollo, 177
salsicce con le rape o spinaci, 114, 115
salt cod: boiled salt cod, 150
　　Florentine salt cod, 151
　　with chickpeas, 150
sauces, 174–85
　　artichoke, 176
　　béchamel, 176
　　broccoli, 182
　　chicken liver, 177
　　country-style tomato, 181
　　pea, 184
　　Pistoiese meat, 178, *179*
　　plain tomato, 185
　　summer, 182, *183*
　　tarragon, 180
sausages: Italian sausages with turnip tops or spinach, 114, *115*

kebabs of wild boar sausages with chicken, 116, *117*

risotto with sausage sauce, 167

Tuscan stuffed onions, 44

veal and sausage envelopes, 122

la schiacciata, 38

schiacciata con l'uva, 200, *200*

sedani alla contadina, 59

seppie con piselli, 146, *147*

sgombro al limone con olive, 160

soups, 8–20

bread and tomato, 10

chicken, 18

clam, 140

cooked water, 18

farmhouse, 19

fish, 148, *149*

miller's, 15

minced (ground) beef, pancetta and vegetables, 11

mussel, 138, *139*

pasta and chickpea, 20

potato, 10

pumpkin, 14

soup of the Moors, 16, *17*

thick bean, 20, *21*

traditional Tuscan fish stew, 163

vegetable, 12, *13*

spaghetti: baker's pasta, 70

spelt: miller's soup, 15

spezzatino alla Fiorentina, 106

spiced milk pudding, 201

spiedini uccelli scappati, 116, *117*

spinach: Italian sausages with, 114, *115*

naked gnocchi, 74

oven-baked gnocchi, *72, 73*

summer pasta salad, 64, *65*

squid with swiss chard, 144, *145*

stracotto alla Fiorentina, 108

stracotto con cipolle, 109

stufato di piselli, 48, *49*

sugo di pomodoro casalinga, 181

summer pasta salad, 64, *65*

summer sauce, 182, *183*

sweet and sour hare, 101

sweet fritters, 196

swiss chard: squid with, 144, *145*

stuffed chicken, 90

sweet swiss chard pie, 197

swiss chard omelette, 32, *33*

swordfish in tomato sauce with potatoes, 158, *159*

tagliata di manzo, 110, 111

tagliatelle: pasta and chickpea soup, 20

tagliatelle al sugo di prosciutto, 78, *79*

tarragon sauce, 180

tipsy chestnuts, 210

tiramisu, 218, 219

toasts, chicken-liver, 28, *29*

tomatoes: Aretina duck, 96

bread and tomato soup, 10

clam soup, 140

cooked water soup, 18

country-style tomato sauce, 181

farmhouse omelette, *34, 35*

Florentine beans, *46, 47*

Florentine beef stew, 106

Florentine braised beef, 108

Florentine salt cod, 151

Florentine tripe, 118

lamb casserole with parsley, 132, *133*

Livornese red mullet, 154, *155*

mussel soup, 138, *139*

noodles with ham sauce, 78, *79*

pasta ribbons with duck sauce, 69

pasta ribbons with mutton sauce, 68

pasta twists with sun-dried tomatoes, 63, *63*

peasant beef meatloaf, 113

peasant-style pasta, 70, *71*

Pistoiese meat sauce, 178, *179*

plain tomato sauce, 185

rabbit in tomato and wine sauce, 100

risotto with cannellini beans, 169

soup of the Moors, 16, *17*

stuffed mussels, *142,* 143

summer pasta salad, 64, *65*

summer sauce, 182, *183*

swordfish in tomato sauce with potatoes, 158, *159*

tomato and bread salad, 38, *39*

Tuscan bean stew, 47

veal and sausage envelopes, 122

veal chops with tomato sauce, 124, *125*

tonno ubriaco, 160, *161*

torta di acciughe, 157

torta di carciofi, 26, 27

torta di ceci, 35

torta di mandorle, 208, 209

torta di riso, 198

torta dolce di bietole, 197

tortelli di patate, 76

triglie alla Livornese, 154, *155*

triglie alla Maremmana, 156

tripe, Florentine, 118

trippa alla Fiorentina, 118

trote alla mugnaia, 162

trout, miller's, 162

truffles: pheasant with black truffles, 99

tuna fish, 'drunken', 160, *161*

turnip tops: Italian sausages with, 114, *115*

sautéed, 48

Tuscan bean stew, 47

Tuscan stuffed onions, 44

uccelletti falsi, 123

vanilla rice cake, 198

veal: farmhouse celery, 59

fool's birds, 123

roast veal, 126, *127*

Tuscan stuffed onions, 44

veal and sausage envelopes, 122

veal chops with tomato sauce, 124, *125*

vegetables, 42–59

baked vegetable lasagne, 80, *81*

farmhouse risotto, 171

farmhouse soup, 19

mixed meat and vegetable fritters, 119

mixed vegetable fritters, 36, *37*

soup of minced (ground) beef, pancetta and vegetables, 11

vegetable soup, 12, *13*

see also artichokes, tomatoes etc

verde fritto, 36, *37*

vongole al pomodoro, 140

whitebait, Livornese, 156

wild boar: kebabs of wild boar sausages with chicken, 116, *117*

roast wild boar, 130

zuccotto alla Fiorentina, 194, 195

zuppa dei mori, 16, *17*

zuppa di cozze, 138, *139*

zuppa di magrograsso, 14

zuppa di patate, 10

zuppa di pesce alla Versigliese, 148, *149*

zuppa di pollo, 18

zuppa paesana, 19

ACKNOWLEDGEMENTS

My grateful thanks go to the following people:

My agent Brian Stone, Colin Webb, Vivien James and Clare Johnson of Pavilion for their encouragement and support, James Murphy for his photography, my wife Letizia, my children Alex, Marietta and Alfonso, my grandchildren Amy and Sidney, the staff at La Famiglia and the many friends and colleagues who have taught me so much over the years and passed on their secrets.